BIG SALADS

THE ULTIMATE FRESH, SATISFYING MEAL, ON ONE PLATE

KAT MEAD

PHOTOGRAPHY BY CATHERINE FRAWLEY

quadrille

BIG SALADS

INTRODUCTION

I love food. I have always loved food! And I have always loved feeding people delicious dishes and seeing the pleasure it brings to their faces and – most importantly – empty plates at the end of a meal. But it's always really exciting to do something new or unexpected; to challenge expectations and inspire people to try something different. Recent trends have led us to think that more dishes are better. So much so that when we have people over we can often fall into the trap of thinking we need to show off with lots of fiddly dishes and that we'll be able to dazzle our guests with the sheer volume of plates we can squeeze onto the table.

But what if there was another way?

What if it could be simpler? What if there was just one dish we had to make? What if we fill that dish with seasonal, colourful, flavoursome ingredients? What if there was more time to spend with your guests? What if everyone shares? It's an interesting thought, isn't it?

What springs to mind when you think of a salad? Limp lettuce? An average vinaigrette? Something served cold? Something you feel you *should* eat rather than want to? Something drab that is served on the side as an afterthought? But what if I told you we can change all of that because the once humble salad is about to get an almighty makeover. Intrigued? Read on.

This is a book packed full of amazing recipes and (hopefully) bucketloads of inspiration to put the previously modest salad firmly centre-stage and challenge the idea of just what a salad has to be.

These are **BIG SALADS**.

These are salads no longer confined to the sidelines; they are the main event. These aren't humble or meagre or tasteless – they are full of flavour, texture and colour with super dressings that bring everything together. They are going to change the way you eat because, as you'll soon discover, everyone loves a big salad. Everyone likes being the person who has made the big salad; the centrepiece of the table that gets people talking, sharing and helping to serve because the platter needs two hands

to hold it. They get people going back greedily for more. They convert non-salad lovers into salad crusaders. You don't need a dozen little dishes – you simply need one of these.

These recipes are expansive generous platters and bowls of food. They are talking-points and showstoppers and they bring you together with everyone lucky enough to be around your table. These are salads for sharing, for fighting and salivating over. It's good, old-fashioned feasting with friends and family, but brought up to date as these recipes are full of flavours from all over the world, inspired by my travels and influences. There are salads for brunch, lunch, dinner and everything in between. They are for everyday and special days. Some are quick, some take a bit of time, but I promise you they are all delicious.

If there was just one thing left to say, it is this. Just get stuck in and use these recipes as a springboard into the idea of Big Salads. There is literally no limit to what they could be – scribble notes on the recipes; dream up new combinations; evolve them; add things and take things away – make them your own and make them firm favourites. Just try them and realise that, when it comes to Big Salads, the rule is simply that there are no rules.

And lastly, if you've made it this far, hopefully you've bought a copy – so thank you dear reader. I really hope you enjoy all these recipes as much as I do. I'd love to see what you cook, so please do share any pictures with me on Instagram @kat_inthekitchen or facebook **Kat In The Kitchen.**

#BIGSALADS

All recipes **FEED 4** people with a healthy appetite, unless otherwise stated.

(V) Vegetarian
(VG) Vegan

SPRING

MELON & CUCUMBER WITH GOAT'S CHEESE, PISTACHIOS & MINT

This is such a fresh, lively spring salad, perfect for those first warmer evenings. Feta has long been a classic to pair with melon, but mix it up by going for a lovely crumbly goat's cheese instead. This is also really easy to make – it's all in the chopping and prep.

200g (7oz) watermelon, deseeded, cut into chunks

200g (7oz) cantaloupe/galia melon, deseeded, cut into chunks

200g (7oz) honeydew (canary) melon, deseeded, cut into chunks

1 large cucumber, peeled, deseeded, cut into chunks

2 tbsp mint leaves, roughly chopped

120g (4¼oz) goat's cheese, crumbled

120g (4¼oz) prosciutto, torn into strips

50g (1¾oz/⅓ cup) pistachios, roughly chopped

FOR THE DRESSING

2 tbsp runny honey

1 lime, zest and juice

2 tbsp pistachio oil

sea salt and fresh pepper

TO SERVE

small handful of mint leaves

Put all the different types of melon and the cucumber into a large mixing bowl, along with the chopped mint. Give everything a gentle mix together.

Make the dressing in a small bowl. Start with the honey, lime zest and juice, and whisk until the honey has fully dissolved. Then add the oil, whisk again, and season to taste.

Pour half the dressing onto the melon and cucumber mix and toss together.

Tip the melon and cucumber into your serving bowl. Crumble over the goat's cheese and wind the prosciutto strips in and around everything. Sprinkle with the pistachio nuts.

Garnish with some fresh mint leaves and drizzle over the rest of the dressing.

TIP This salad can easily be made vegetarian by omitting the prosciutto.

PEA, ASPARAGUS, EGGS & LEMON LABNEH (V)

Asparagus has a relatively short season in the northern hemisphere – usually around mid-April to June – and I always find myself eating it greedily during that time to make the most of it. This salad is fresh, tangy, creamy and crunchy and has a little heat to round it all off. While you can buy labneh, it's never quite as delicious or as much fun as making your own. This quantity makes enough for two salads (or use the remainder as part of some mezze, or spread on toast with a drizzle of olive oil). If you store the leftovers in a clean, airtight container in the fridge, it will easily last a week.

FOR THE LABNEH (MAKES 450G/1LB)
500g (1lb 2oz/2 cups) Greek yogurt
300g (10½oz/1¼ cups) natural
  (plain) yogurt
1 tsp sea salt
1 lemon, zest and juice

FOR THE SALAD
400g (14oz) asparagus
240g (8½oz/1 cup) fresh (or frozen) peas
200g (7oz) sugar snap peas
2½ tbsp pumpkin seeds
2½ tbsp sunflower seeds

2 tbsp golden flaxseed
2 tbsp white wine vinegar
4 eggs, at room temperature
100g (3½oz) pea shoots

FOR THE DRESSING
2 tbsp extra virgin olive oil
1 tbsp lemon juice
sea salt and freshly ground black pepper

TO SERVE
1 tbsp extra virgin olive oil
1 tsp chilli flakes (crushed chilli)

Start the labneh the day before you plan to make the salad. Put the two yogurts, salt, lemon zest and juice into a large bowl and mix everything together well. Line another large bowl with a big piece of muslin (about 40 x 80cm/20 x 40in), folded to double thickness, and drape the corners over the edge of the bowl. Use a spatula to scoop the yogurt mix into the muslin.

Tie the muslin corners together, first to make a tight bundle around the yogurt, and then again to make a loop so that you can hang up the bundle. I find a kitchen cupboard handle works well for this or you could use your kitchen tap; just make sure it's in a cool spot out of direct sunlight. Place a bowl underneath to catch the whey and juice that will start to drip. And that's it. Leave it to do its thing overnight, or for 6–8 hours. The longer you leave it, the firmer it will get. *Continued overleaf*

PEA, ASPARAGUS, EGGS & LEMON LABNEH

When you are ready to make the salad, preheat the oven to 190°C/170°C fan/375°F/gas mark 5 and bring a large pan of water to the boil with a steamer basket and lid.

Snap the asparagus ends off at their natural breaking point. Slice the thicker stems in half lengthways and leave the thinner ones whole. Steam for 1 minute before adding the peas and sugar snaps. Continue to steam for another 3–4 minutes. Remove and plunge into a large bowl of iced water. This will stop the veg cooking and preserve the amazing shades of green.

Line a roasting tin with baking parchment. Scatter all the seeds into the tin and pop it into the oven for 7 minutes. Then take the tin out and give it a shake to move the seeds around; return to the oven for another 5 minutes. The seeds should turn a lovely golden brown and the pumpkin seeds will have started to pop open. Remove and set aside to cool.

Bring another large deep pan of water to the boil and add the white wine vinegar. Crack each egg into a little cup or ramekin (four in total). Once the water has come to the boil, reduce the heat to a gentle simmer. Gently swirl the water with a spoon to make a vortex in the middle. Quickly add an egg to the side of the pan – the water will pull it into the middle. Repeat with the other eggs until they are all in – you need to do this as quickly as possible so they cook evenly!

Let the eggs gently poach for 3 minutes for a runny yolk. Carefully lift them out with a slotted spoon and drain on some paper towel.

Take a large serving plate and scatter it with the pea shoots. Drain the vegetables and transfer them to a mixing bowl. Add the ingredients for the dressing, season to taste, and mix it all together with your hands to coat the vegetables. Carefully arrange the veg on top of the peashoots. Crumble over half the lemon labneh and lay the poached eggs on top.

Finally scatter over the toasted seeds and drizzle over any dressing left in the bowl from the veg. Serve with another drizzle of extra virgin olive oil and a sprinkle of chilli flakes.

TIP The peashoots, steamed veg, toasted seeds and dressing make a great vegan salad in their own right.

AVOCADO, QUAIL EGGS & BUTTERHEAD LETTUCE (V)

This is a great salad to throw together when you have people coming round at short notice. It's super-quick – and soft-boiled quail eggs make even the simplest dish look impressive! Anyone would think you'd been planning this for days…

12 quail eggs (if you can't get quail eggs, use 6 small eggs), at room temperature
200g (7oz) thin rice noodles
100g (3½oz) butterhead lettuce, separated into leaves
2 cucumbers
1 red onion, sliced into thin crescents
150g (5½oz) on-the-vine cherry tomatoes, halved

2 avocados

FOR THE DRESSING
2 tbsp extra virgin olive oil
1 tbsp lemon juice
2 tsp poppy seeds
1 garlic clove, finely grated (minced)
½ tsp sea salt

Bring a medium pan of water to the boil. Carefully add the quail eggs – I slide them in using a big spoon – and cook for 2½ minutes. Run them under really cold water for at least 5 minutes to stop them cooking any more. Peel and set aside.

Cook the rice noodles according to the packet instructions (usually simmering or soaking in boiling water for 3 or 4 minutes). Drain and run under cold water to stop them cooking further, then set aside.

Place the lettuce leaves in a large mixing bowl. Peel the cucumber into long ribbons straight into the bowl. You want to avoid the seeds as much as possible, so discard the centre when you get to it.

Add the onion and tomatoes. Cut the avocados in half, remove the stone and use a spoon to scoop out the flesh – this all goes into the bowl too. Finally, add the rice noodles.

Mix all the ingredients for the dressing together – shaking them up in an clean jam jar is a great way of doing this – and pour over the salad in the mixing bowl. Give it a good mix – don't worry about breaking up the avocado, it all just mingles with the dressing and coats the noodles. Transfer everything to a big platter, arranging the noodles and cucumber ribbons into beautiful swirls. Cut the quail eggs in half and dot them over and around the salad.

pictured on page 18 (top)

WARM TIGER PRAWN COCKTAIL SALAD

This is a rather decadent take on the classic prawn cocktail – a firm favourite in our house in the 1980s, when I fell in love with the creamy avocado and tangy thousand island combo. Using tiger prawns gives this real substance, as they are almost meaty, but you could easily use any other large raw prawn instead. Share, but only if you want to!

600g (1lb 5oz) raw tiger prawns (shrimp),
  approximately 20
1 tbsp olive oil
2 tbsp tamarind paste
juice of 1 lemon
1 romaine lettuce, shredded
75g (2¾oz) lamb's lettuce
1 cucumber, peeled and cut into chunks
2 avocados

FOR THE THOUSAND ISLAND DRESSING
2 tbsp mayonnaise

2 tbsp ketchup
2 tbsp horseradish sauce
1 tbsp cider vinegar
1 garlic clove, finely grated (minced)
8 cornichons, finely chopped
½ tsp hot pepper sauce
sea salt and freshly ground black pepper

TO SERVE
lemon wedges
small handful of chives, finely chopped
pinch of paprika

First, prep the prawns. Prawns always look more dramatic when you leave some of the shell on. Very carefully remove the shell from the body, leaving the head and tail on. De-vein the prawn by gently slicing down its back – you should be able to see the vein and pull it out.

Heat a large frying or sauté pan over a high heat. Add the oil and then the prawns. Keep tossing the pan to turn the prawns so that they cook evenly. After about 4 minutes, add the tamarind paste. Swirl the prawns in the sauce so that it sizzles and bubbles and starts to coat them in a delicious sticky glaze. Squeeze over the lemon juice and keep cooking until the prawns are all pink, curled and cooked through – it should take less than 5 minutes. Remove from the heat while you assemble the salad.

Whisk all the dressing ingredients together in a small bowl, seasoning to taste. Place all the lettuce and the cucumber into a large mixing bowl and add half the dressing. Mix together before you transfer to a platter to serve. Halve the avocados and scoop the flesh straight on top. Add the prawns to the centre of the platter, along with some lemon wedges to serve, and the rest of the dressing on the side for dunking the prawns into. Finish with a sprinkling of chopped chives and a pinch of paprika.

pictured on previous page

GRILLED ROMAINE CHICKEN CAESAR WITH AVOCADO

This is a Caesar salad with a little twist but it should hit the spot for anyone looking for a classic. Super-delicious when it's made with a fresh roast chicken, but you could always use pre-cooked chicken instead to speed things up.

1 chicken, about 1.5kg (3lb 5oz)

4 tbsp olive oil

½ tsp garlic salt

10 streaky bacon rashers (slices)

2 romaine lettuces, cut into 6 wedges
   through the root

200g (7oz) on-the-vine cherry tomatoes
   halved

4 slices of sourdough bread, 1.5cm
   (⅝in) thick

1 large garlic clove

2 avocados

150g (5½oz) fresh anchovy fillets
   (if you can't get fresh anchovies use
   marinated instead)

sea salt and freshly ground black pepper

FOR THE CAESAR DRESSING

1 garlic clove, roughly chopped

3 canned anchovies, roughly chopped

2 tsp lemon juice

1 tsp water

1 tsp Dijon mustard

2 egg yolks

150ml (5fl oz/scant ⅔ cup) light olive oil

30g Parmesan cheese, roughly grated
   (shredded)

sea salt and black pepper

Preheat the oven to 210°C/190°C fan/410°F/gas mark 6. Line a roasting tin with baking parchment, sit the chicken on it, drizzle over about 1 tablespoon of olive oil and sprinkle over the garlic salt. Roast in the oven for 50–55 minutes.

Heat a large frying pan (skillet) over a medium heat and add the bacon. Turn occasionally. Once it's super-crispy, after about 10 minutes, transfer to some paper towels to absorb the fat. Once cool, blitz in a food processor to a fine crumb. Set aside for later.

Use a small food processor to make the dressing. Add the garlic, anchovies, lemon juice, water, Dijon and egg yolks, and blitz to a smooth paste. Then, with the engine running, slowly add the olive oil as if you were making a mayonnaise: a few drops at a time to start with, building up to a thin, steady stream. When it's all incorporated, transfer to a bowl and mix in the Parmesan and season to taste. Go easy on the salt, as both the anchovies and the cheese will take care of that, but lots of black pepper is lovely. *Continued overleaf*

GRILLED ROMAINE CHICKEN CAESAR WITH AVOCADO

Heat a griddle pan and when it's hot, brush the cut sides of the lettuce wedges with another tablespoon of the olive oil and place them on the griddle. Leave to char for about 2 minutes before you turn them over and do the other side. When you have some good char lines, put the lettuce wedges on a chopping board and cut the root off so the leaves fall apart. Slide them into a large mixing bowl along with the cherry tomatoes.

Pop the slices of sourdough in a roasting tin and into the hot oven with the chicken for 6 minutes. Remove from the oven and gently rub the garlic all over one side of the toast. Cut into chunks, return to the roasting tin and cover with the remaining two tablespoons of oil. Pop it back into the oven for another 6–7 minutes until golden brown and crisp.

The chicken will probably be ready at this point, so take it out of the oven and allow it to rest for 10 minutes before shredding (with or without the skin – it's up to you). Add to the mixing bowl with 4 tablespoons of the Caesar dressing and lightly mix it all together.

Heap the chicken onto your serving plate. Stone and slice the avocados and pile them on top, along with the anchovies and croutons. Sprinkle with the bacon crumb and devour. Creamy, salty, warm, crunchy goodness in every mouthful.

SPROUTING BROCCOLI & BUCKWHEAT WITH MISO (VG)

This is a heavenly salad: big and bold and – green! Miso has such a deep umami flavour that goes so well with the nutty buckwheat and more earthy, bitter broccoli. The salad is just hugely, hugely delicious and a big hoorah for the wonder veg that is broccoli.

180g (6¼oz/generous 1 cup) buckwheat

300g (10½oz) sprouting broccoli

200g (7oz) green (string) beans

2 tsp coriander (cilantro) leaves,
   roughly chopped

1 small red onion, very thinly sliced

100g (3½oz) rocket (arugula)

2 avocados

FOR THE MISO DRESSING

4 tbsp extra virgin olive oil

2 tbsp red miso paste

1 tbsp soy sauce

1 tbsp mirin

1 tbsp lime juice

1 garlic clove, finely grated (minced)

2cm (¾in) ginger, peeled and finely
   grated (minced)

TO SERVE

1 sheet of nori seaweed

1 tbsp sesame seeds

2 jalapeño chillies, thinly sliced (optional)

Tip the buckwheat into a large saucepan and cover with cold water. Bring the water up to the boil and then simmer, cooking according to the packet instructions (usually around 8–10 minutes).

Meanwhile, bring another pan of water to the boil with a steamer basket and lid. Add the broccoli and the green beans, and steam until just tender – about 5–6 minutes.

When everything is cooked, remove from the heat and drain. Place the buckwheat into a large mixing bowl. Mix all the ingredients for the dressing in a small bowl or jug and whisk well. Add half of the dressing to the buckwheat along with the chopped coriander, onion and rocket. Stone and roughly chop the avocados, and add these, mixing well.

Pour the buckwheat mix out onto your serving dish, layering up the broccoli and green beans in the middle. Drizzle over the rest of the dressing, crumble over the seaweed and sprinkle on the sesame seeds. If you want to give it a little heat, add the jalapeños too!

pictured on page 28 (left)

DUKKAH-CRUSTED FLAKED COD & CRUSHED POTATOES

Jersey royals just shout spring. There are few things more delicious than that first fluffy, buttery bite but combine Jersey royals with some quick pan-cooked cod and you have a simple, light potato salad. Perfect for those lengthening spring evenings.

600g (1lb 5oz) cod loin, ideally in
   two evenly sized pieces
2 tbsp light olive oil
1kg (2lb 4oz) Jersey royal potatoes, washed
   but skin on
200g (7oz/1⅔ cups) fresh (or frozen) peas
200g (7oz) sugar snap peas
100g (3½oz/scant ½ cup) butter, room
   temperature
25ml (1fl oz/5 tsp) extra virgin
   olive oil
1 garlic clove, finely grated (minced)
bunch of spring onions (scallions), sliced

2 tsp flat-leaf parsley, roughly chopped
1 lemon, zest and juice
sea salt and freshly ground black pepper

FOR THE DUKKAH
30g (1oz/¼ cup) blanched hazelnuts
2 tbsp sesame seeds
1 tbsp coriander seeds
1 tbsp cumin seeds
1 tsp sea salt
½ tsp freshly ground black pepper

First, make the dukkah. Preheat your oven to 180°C/160°C fan/350°F/gas mark 4 and place everything except the salt and pepper into a roasting tin. Toast in the oven for about 10 minutes, shaking once halfway through to move everything round. The nuts will turn golden brown and the spices will pop and become aromatic. Transfer everything to a spice blender or small food processor. Pulse until the nuts are broken down and the seeds have become more of a powder. You can store any leftovers in an airtight container to use another time – it will keep for at least a month.

Find a dish that the cod fits in and put in half of the light olive oil and as much dukkah as you need to roughly cover the fish (about 2–3 tbsp). Pat the fish dry and then rub it around in the dish to coat it in the oil and dukkah. Set aside.

You want all the potatoes to be roughly the same size so they cook evenly – halve any bigger ones, leaving the rest whole. Place in a large saucepan and cover with cold water and a good pinch of salt. Put over a high heat and bring to the boil, then reduce to a simmer and cook for around 20 minutes until tender (test with the tip of a knife). When they are ready, remove from the heat and drain in a colander. Leave them to steam themselves dry.

Turn the oven up to 200°C/180°C fan/400°F/gas mark 6.

Bring another pan of water to the boil with a steamer basket and lid. Add the peas and sugar snaps and steam for 4 minutes or so until cooked al dente. Drain and set aside.

Transfer the potatoes to an ovenproof dish that you can take straight to the table. Add the butter and the extra virgin olive oil. Mix everything together roughly and pop into the oven for 10 minutes. Remove the dish and turn everything over, pressing down with the back of a spoon to break open the potatoes so they catch even more yummy butter and oil. Return to the oven for 10 minutes. Then add the peas, sugar snaps and garlic, and return to the oven for a final 3 minutes. Turn the oven off, open the door a crack to release some of the heat and leave the dish in there to stay warm while you cook the fish.

Heat a frying pan (skillet) with the remaining light olive oil over a medium–high heat. Cook the fish for 3 minutes, then carefully flip over and cook for another 2 minutes. Remove the fish from the pan and leave it to rest on a board.

Using the back of a fork, press down on the cod to break it into lovely chunks and flakes of tender, pearlescent fish. Take the roasting dish out of the oven and arrange the fish over the top of the potatoes.

Scatter over the sliced spring onions and parsley. Grate over the lemon zest and finish with a little squeeze of lemon juice.

pictured overleaf (centre)

TIP This salad can easily be made vegetarian by omitting the cod.

EGG, ASPARAGUS & CONFIT GARLIC AIOLI

I love eggs and asparagus together – they are a classic combination for a reason – but with the spinach and garlic aioli they become totally moreish. Add the salty chorizo and crispy breadcrumbs, and the salad goes from ordinary to extraordinary. I promise, this is so quick (once the confit garlic is made) and so good it will become a firm favourite.

1 garlic bulb
150ml (5fl oz/scant ⅔ cup) olive oil, plus
  1 tsp to coat
150g (5½oz) cooking chorizo, finely diced
100g (3½oz/2 cups) fresh breadcrumbs
4 eggs, at room temperature
400g (14oz) asparagus, trimmed
100g (3½oz) baby leaf spinach
50g (1¾oz) pea shoots
sea salt and freshly ground black pepper

FOR THE AIOLI
4 confit garlic cloves (see method)
2 egg yolks
1 tbsp water
1 tbsp lemon juice
100ml (3½fl oz/scant ½ cup) extra virgin
  olive oil
50ml (1¾fl oz/scant ¼ cup) light olive oil

Preheat your oven to 120°C/100°C fan/250°F/gas mark ½. First make the confit garlic. Break the garlic bulb into cloves and place them (skin on) in a small ovenproof dish, in which they fit snugly. Cover with the olive oil and pop into the oven for 1 hour. You don't want the oil to bubble and boil, so do check it occasionally. Remove from the oven and leave to cool to room temperature in the oil. You can store the garlic, covered in the oil, for up to two weeks in the fridge. Plus, you have delicious ready-made garlic oil, perfect for salad dressings or to rub onto chicken or lamb before roasting.

Heat a large frying pan (skillet) over a medium–high heat and add the chorizo. It will very quickly start to cook and release some of its oils. Keep the chorizo moving around so it is fried on all sides, and keep breaking it down with the back of your wooden spoon as you move it so the pieces get more and more crumb-like. After about 5 minutes, add the breadcrumbs and stir to get them all mixed into the oil and chorizo. Keep cooking until the breadcrumbs and chorizo are crisp – probably another 4–5 minutes. You may need to reduce the heat so nothing burns before it crisps. Tip onto some paper towel to soak up any excess oil and set aside.

To make the aioli, squeeze four garlic cloves from their skins and put them in a small food processor, along with the egg yolks, water and lemon juice. Blitz everything together until smooth and then very slowly start to add the oil a few drops at a time. Once you have about half the oil incorporated, you can start to pour it in a thin, steady stream. This will probably make more than you want but the aioli will keep in an airtight jar or container in the fridge for at least a week.

Bring a large pan of water to the boil. Slide in the eggs carefully and cook for 6½ minutes, so you have lovely soft, runny middles. Place a steamer basket on top and steam the asparagus for around 4 minutes until just tender.

Place the cooked asparagus in a large mixing bowl and run the eggs under cold water until cool enough to handle.

Add the spinach and pea shoots to the mixing bowl and toss them together with the teaspoon of olive oil – so they are just coated. Transfer everything to a big plate and add dollops of the aioli. Peel the eggs, slice into halves and arrange them on top. Sprinkle over the crispy chorizo breadcrumbs.

<u>pictured on previous page (top right)</u>

TIP This salad can easily be made vegetarian by omitting the chorizo and frying the breadcrumbs in 1 tablespoon of olive oil.

SHAVED FENNEL & CANNELLINI BEAN (VG)

This salad is super-fresh and delicious. You can also make it in advance if you need to – just add the dressing at the last moment. And while it is fabulous on its own, you could partner it with pretty much any meat or fish if you want to feed more than four people.

2 fennel bulbs, thinly sliced on a mandolin

2 x 400g (14oz) cans cannellini beans, drained and rinsed (about 460g/1lb total drained weight)

2 red or ruby grapefruits, segmented, juice reserved

1 red onion, finely sliced

100g (3½oz) pomegranate seeds

60g (2¼oz) rocket (arugula)

FOR THE DRESSING
4 tbsp extra virgin olive oil

2 tbsp grapefruit juice

1 lemon, zest and juice

2 tsp flat-leaf parsley leaves, finely chopped

1 tsp dill leaves, finely chopped

1 tsp coriander (cilantro) leaves, finely chopped

sea salt and fresh pepper

TO SERVE
small handful of flat-leaf parsley leaves

4 slices of sourdough bread

Put the fennel, cannellini beans and grapefruit segments into a large mixing bowl. Add the red onion, pomegranate and rocket.

Make the dressing by adding all the ingredients into a small mixing bowl or jam jar – start with just one tablespoon of lemon juice and add more to taste. Whisk or shake it together well, before pouring all over the salad. Use your hands to mix and coat everything evenly.

Turn out the salad into a large serving bowl. Top with the parsley and serve with some bread to soak up all the delicious juices.

pictured on page 29 (bottom right)

FENNEL & ORANGE SALAD WITH CARAMELISED PECANS (V)

This really bridges the gap between winter and spring by using the last crops of fennel and the first zingy sunshine oranges. A burst of sour notes from the pomegranate seeds balances the sweetness of the caramelised pecans.

60g (2¼oz/¼ cup) granulated sugar

2 tbsp water

20g (¾oz/1½ tbsp) unsalted butter

80g (2¾oz/¾ cup) pecan nuts

150g (5½oz/¾ cup) pearl barley

80g (2¾oz) rocket (arugula)

40g (1½oz) watercress, tough stalks discarded

2 fennel bulbs, thinly sliced on a mandolin

3 medium oranges, segmented

100g (3½oz) radishes, thinly sliced on a mandolin

100g (3½oz) pomegranate seeds

FOR THE DRESSING

2 tbsp olive oil

1 tbsp orange juice

2 tsp Dijon mustard

2 tsp cider vinegar

sea salt and freshly ground black pepper

Line a baking sheet with baking parchment. Place the sugar in a medium saucepan over medium heat. The sugar will slowly start to melt, at which point you need to brush the sides of the pan with the water to ensure that there are no loose grains of sugar, which could crystallise your caramel. Once the sugar has completely dissolved, it will start to turn golden: wait for it to go a deep gold colour, like syrup. At that point, carefully add the butter and swirl the pan to combine. It may spit and sputter so be careful not to burn yourself. Quickly tip in the nuts and stir, using a metal spoon, to coat them in the caramel, then tip the nuts onto the baking sheet and spread them out to cool.

Rinse the barley in a sieve, then place in a saucepan, cover with cold water and bring to the boil. Reduce the heat and simmer for 50–60 minutes, until it is al dente (with just a little bite). Drain and leave to steam itself dry for a couple of minutes.

Mix all the dressing ingredients together by shaking them in an clean jam jar and season to taste.

Now it's an assembly job. Add the rocket, watercress, fennel and orange segments to a large mixing bowl, along with the radishes, pomegranate seeds and cooked barley. Pour the dressing over the salad and toss everything together to make sure it's all coated. Spread the salad out onto a large platter and crumble the caramelised pecans over the top.

pictured overleaf (bottom)

SWEET & SOUR RICE NOODLES, EDAMAME & CABBAGE (VG)

This is a real go-to recipe for me when I'm after something quick but comforting – everyone loves noodles. Using rice noodles here keeps everything feeling light and the salad should be really crunchy and full of flavour. Prawns or some griddled chicken would be a great addition to this if you wanted to stretch it out even more. This salad is crunchy, sweet and sour, and it makes your mouth dance. There won't be any leftovers.

1 small pineapple
150g (5½oz) rice noodles
3 carrots, peeled and julienned
2 yellow (bell) peppers, thinly sliced
½ Savoy cabbage, shredded
200g (7oz) edamame beans
300g (10½oz) bean sprouts
1 tbsp olive oil

FOR THE SWEET AND SOUR SAUCE
1 tsp light olive oil
3cm (1in) ginger, peeled and finely chopped
4 garlic cloves, finely grated (minced)
100ml (3½fl oz/scant ½ cup) pineapple juice

50ml (1¾fl oz/scant ¼ cup) ketchup
50ml (1¾fl oz/scant ¼ cup) rice wine vinegar
2½ tbsp maple syrup
1 tbsp dark brown sugar
1 tbsp cornflour (cornstarch), dissolved in 2 tbsp cold water

TO SERVE
4 spring onions (scallions), sliced on the diagonal
2 red chillies, thinly sliced
small handful of coriander (cilantro) leaves
lime wedges

First make the sauce. Heat the oil in a small wok or saucepan on a medium–high heat. Add the ginger and garlic and fry for 20–30 seconds until they release their wonderful aromas, stirring all the time so nothing burns. Add the pineapple juice, ketchup, rice wine vinegar, maple syrup and sugar. Stir everything together really, really well and let it come to the boil. At this point, add the cornflour mix. Keep stirring and after a few seconds the sauce will suddenly thicken. Cook for another 30 seconds or so, then remove from the heat and leave to cool down.

Cut three slices from your pineapple, each about 1.5cm (½in) thick, and carefully remove the core and rind, so you have rings. Heat a griddle pan on a medium–high heat and when it's hot, add the pineapple. You should get some sticky brown caramelisation after about 2 minutes or so, then flip each ring over and grill on the other side. Remove from the pan, cut into chunks and set aside.

Cook the rice noodles according to the packet instructions (usually simmering or soaking in boiling water for 3 or 4 minutes). Drain into a colander and run under cold water for a few minutes to stop them cooking further.

Mix all the veg in a large mixing bowl. Heat the olive oil in a wok and then tip in the mixed veg and stir-fry for 2 minutes. Add the noodles and the pineapple chunks. Add the sweet and sour sauce and mix everything together until just heated through.

Heap the noodles into a big serving dish. Scatter with the spring onions and chilli. Sprinkle the coriander over the top and serve with big wedges of lime for that extra zingy kick.

pictured on page 34 (top left)

PAPAYA SALAD WITH COCONUT-POACHED CHICKEN

This hot, sour, salty, crunchy and nutty salad is eaten all across south-east Asia and, to me, it tastes like sunshine. The addition of coconut-poached chicken turns it from a simple side to the main event – and what an event it is. Pile it high and watch it just disappear.

2 chicken breasts, skinless
400ml (14fl oz/1⅔ cup) coconut milk
1 lemongrass stalk, outer leaves removed, finely chopped
6 kaffir lime leaves
3 garlic cloves, roughly chopped
2–4 red bird's eye chillies, finely sliced (start with 2 and see how you go!)
300g (10½oz) green (string) beans, sliced into 2-cm (¾-in) lengths
20 on-the-vine cherry tomatoes, halved
3 green papayas, peeled and coarsely grated

60g (2¼oz/generous ⅓ cup) roasted peanuts, chopped

FOR THE DRESSING
2 limes, zest and juice
1 tbsp dried shrimp paste
2 tbsp fish sauce
2 tbsp palm sugar

TO SERVE
handful of Thai basil leaves
lime wedges

Place the chicken breasts into a small sauté pan and cover with the coconut milk – if it doesn't quite cover the chicken, just top up with a little water. Add the lemongrass and four of the kaffir lime leaves. Place the pan over a low heat and bring the coconut milk to a gentle simmer. Poach the chicken for 12 minutes, then turn off the heat and leave the chicken to cool in the coconut milk, so it continues to absorb flavour from all the aromatics.

While the chicken is cooking, put the garlic in a large pestle and mortar and bash to a paste. Add the chillies and the last two kaffir lime leaves and bash again so they start to release their oils.

Add the green beans and cherry tomatoes and bash again to bruise them. If you don't have a big enough pestle and mortar, you could do this in batches and transfer to a mixing bowl as you go. Or just use the end of a rolling pin in a mixing bowl! The idea is to get all the flavours and juices mingling together – use a spoon or spatula to turn everything over and get it well mixed.

Add the papayas to the pestle and mortar and pound. Keep turning and blending as you go. Add the chopped nuts and stir through. Set to one side.

In a small bowl, mix the lime juice (keep the zest for later), shrimp paste, fish sauce and sugar and stir until the sugar has dissolved. Give it a taste — it should be primarily sharp, then salty with a hint of sweetness. You can always add a little more of one or other of the ingredients to balance it to your taste.

Remove the chicken from the pan and gently shred it using two forks. (You can discard the poaching liquid or use it as the base for a soup another day.)

Transfer everything from the mortar to a large mixing bowl and add the dressing. Mix together well. Tip everything out onto a large platter and spread out. Place a huge mound of the coconut chicken on top and scatter over some fresh Thai basil leaves and the lime zest.

Serve with some lime wedges and a nice cold beer.

pictured on page 35 (right)

ROAST ONION, BEETROOT & RADICCHIO (VG)

This is delicious in early spring – just as radicchio really comes into season. It's dark and deeply savoury – almost meaty, punctuated with refreshing bursts of pomegranate and dill. Salad is not just for summer and this one proves it.

400g (14oz) beetroot (beets), peeled and
    cut into wedges
3 tbsp olive oil
2 red onions, peeled and cut into 6 wedges
2 brown onions, peeled and cut into 6
    wedges
200ml (7fl oz/generous ¾ cup) balsamic
    vinegar
1 radicchio, cut into quarters through
    the root

50g (1¾oz) watercress, tough stalks
    discarded
100g (3½oz/⅔ cup) pomegranate seeds
50g (1¾oz/⅓ cup) hazelnuts, toasted,
    roughly chopped
small handful of dill leaves
sea salt and freshly ground black pepper

Preheat the oven to 200°C/180°C fan/400°F/gas mark 6. Place the beetroot wedges into a large roasting tin, drizzle over 2 tablespoons of the oil and season well. Use your hands to mix and get everything coated in the oil, and then pop into the hot oven. After 30 minutes, remove the tray and turn everything over. Add the onion wedges and stir to coat in the oil and seasoning. Return to the oven for another 20–25 minutes, until the beetroot are tender and the onions golden brown.

Meanwhile, put the balsamic vinegar in a small saucepan on a medium heat. You need to reduce it by half its original volume, so it becomes syrupy in texture with a sweeter, more intense flavour (it reminds me of toffee apples). This will take around 20 minutes on a gentle rolling boil. Check on it often as you don't want it to boil over. When it is done, remove from the heat and leave to cool.

Heat a griddle pan on a medium–high heat and brush the cut sides of the radicchio with the remaining oil. When the griddle is hot, add the radicchio, cut side down, and cook for 2 minutes until it has lightly charred, then flip it onto its other cut side and cook for another 2 minutes. Try not to check on it too often. Once you have some good char lines, remove from the pan and place on a chopping board. Cut off the root so the leaves separate. Pull them apart and lay them on a big plate.

Top with the watercress and roasted veg. Sprinkle with the pomegranate seeds and the chopped hazelnuts. Drizzle over some of the balsamic reduction, season and scatter the dill leaves on top.

BAKED RHUBARB, FETA, BEETROOT & FLATBREAD (V)

This recipe is in the Spring chapter as it is particularly delicious (and beautiful) with the first forced shoots of pink rhubarb, but any rhubarb works. The salad combines some ingredients that you might not think go together, but trust me, they really do! It is one of my all-time favourites – salty, sweet, sharp, creamy and deeply satisfying. And don't worry, making the flatbreads is really simple (or you could buy some to make it easier).

200g (7oz) rhubarb, cut into 2-cm
  (¾-in) chunks
2 x 200-g (7-oz) packets of feta
120g (4¼oz) beetroot (beets), peeled and
  cut into small wedges
60ml (2fl oz/¼ cup) runny honey
1 tbsp olive oil
small handful of thyme sprigs
1 tsp chilli flakes (crushed chilli)
150g (5½oz) mixed green leaves
50g (1¾oz/generous ½ cup) flaked (sliced)
  almonds, toasted
100g (3½oz/1 cup) walnuts, toasted
freshly ground black pepper

FOR THE FLATBREADS
180g (6¼oz/1½ cups) plain
  (all-purpose) flour
80–100ml (2¾fl oz–3½fl oz/⅓ cup–scant
  ½ cup) water, at room temperature
olive oil, for brushing
sea salt

FOR THE DRESSING
juice from the beets and feta
1 tbsp extra virgin olive oil
sea salt and freshly ground black pepper

TO SERVE
extra virgin olive oil
freshly ground black pepper

Preheat the oven to 200°C/180°C fan/400°F/gas mark 6 and line a roasting tin with baking parchment. Lay a large sheet of foil (big enough to make a parcel) on a baking sheet.

Spread out the rhubarb in a single layer on the baking paper in the roasting tin. Place the two blocks of feta side by side in the middle of the foil on the baking sheet. Scatter the beetroot on and around the feta. Drizzle over the honey and oil, scatter with the thyme sprigs and chilli flakes, and season with a little pepper (you won't need to add salt as the feta is salty enough).

Fold up the sides of the foil to make a parcel and pop both trays in the oven with the feta on the top shelf. Bake the rhubarb for 15 minutes and the feta for 25 minutes. *Continued overleaf*

BAKED RHUBARB, FETA, BEETROOT & FLATBREAD

While everything is in the oven, make the flatbreads. Put the flour into a large mixing bowl with a big pinch of salt. Add 80ml of the water, then, using one hand, start to mix it together into a dough. If it feels a bit dry and crumbly, add a little more water. Transfer the rough dough to your work surface and knead for 4–5 minutes until it becomes smooth and elastic. Keep the dough covered with a clean, damp cloth until you are ready to use it.

Heat a large frying pan (skillet) over a medium heat. Divide the dough into four round balls. Roll one ball out as thinly as you can and brush one side with a light coating of oil. Carefully transfer it to the dry frying pan, oiled side down, and cook for a couple of minutes. Brush the top of the flatbread with oil while it's in the pan, before flipping over and cooking for another couple of minutes. You should see some air bubbles appearing. Repeat this process until you have made all four flatbreads.

By this point, the rhubarb and the feta should be deliciously baked. Carefully open the foil packet (be mindful of the steam inside) and discard the thyme.

Assemble the salad by tearing the flatbreads into quarters to make a base over your serving platter. Put the leaves into a mixing bowl, pour over the cooking juices from the feta parcel along with the oil for the dressing and a little seasoning, and toss to coat. Arrange the leaves on top of the flatbread and then add the rhubarb. Break the feta into chunks and scatter, along with the beetroot, over the leaves, then add the toasted nuts. Finally, drizzle over some extra virgin olive oil and a twist of pepper.

Scoop up your salad, rhubarb, feta, beetroot and nuts with your flatbread, close your eyes and enjoy.

DINOSAUR EGGS WITH EDAMAME & VEG NOODLES (V)

This salad is just so simple and full of interesting flavours. It's also a lovely, light salad as it uses spiralised cucumber and courgette instead of a traditional noodle. The 'dinosaur eggs' are always an amazing talking point; not only do they look incredible but they become firmer in texture than normal boiled eggs as they cure.

4 eggs, at room temperature
100ml (3½fl oz/scant ½ cup) soy sauce
200g (7oz) edamame beans (frozen are fine)
200g (7oz) baby broad (fava) beans
1 cucumber
2 courgettes (zucchini)
bunch of spring onions (scallions), sliced
1 red chilli, finely chopped
1 tsp black sesame seeds
1 tsp white sesame seeds, toasted
vegetable oil, for shallow frying
5 echalion (banana) shallots, thinly and evenly sliced

FOR THE DRESSING
10g (⅓oz) pickled ginger, finely chopped
2 tsp coriander (cilantro) leaves, finely chopped
1 garlic clove, very finely grated (minced)
2 tbsp soy sauce
2 tbsp toasted sesame oil
1 tbsp mirin
1 tbsp rice wine vinegar

TO SERVE
radish shoots
chilli flakes (crushed chilli)
white sesame seeds, toasted (optional)
black sesame seeds (optional)

Make the dinosaur eggs first. Bring a large pan of water to the boil and slowly slide in the eggs. Cook them for around 7 minutes for a slightly soft centre. Once they are cooked, run them under cold water to stop them cooking any more. Then gently tap and roll the eggs one by one on a worktop. You want to crack the shells, but you're not going to peel them – yet!

Put them into a small airtight container, in which they just fit snugly, and pour over enough soy sauce to cover them. Press a paper towel down on top of the eggs to make sure they evenly soak up the soy sauce. Place the lid on and leave for about 6 hours. The longer you leave them, the more 'pickled' they become. Start with less time and build up to your own preference; I like to leave them overnight.

Continued overleaf

DINOSAUR EGGS WITH EDAMAME & VEG NOODLES

When you are ready to make your salad, bring a pan of water to the boil with a steamer basket and lid. Steam the edamame and broad beans for about 5 minutes. Drain and rinse under cold water to make sure they stop cooking and stay a really vibrant green. Gently squeeze the broad bean skins so the bright green beans pop out of their tough, bitter outer layer. Place all the beans in a mixing bowl.

Next, spiralise the cucumber and courgettes (peel into ribbons if you don't have a spiraliser), and add to the bowl, along with the spring onions, chilli and sesame seeds. Mix everything together and set aside.

Pour about 3cm (1in) of vegetable oil into a saucepan and place over a medium–high heat. The oil is ready when you add a cube of bread and it sizzles gently. Add the shallots and deep-fry for 5–6 minutes until they're a lovely crisp, golden brown. You will need to stir them occasionally to make sure they cook evenly. Using a metal slotted spoon, lift them out onto a baking sheet lined with paper towels to absorb the excess oil.

Combine all the ingredients for the dressing (by shaking them in an clean jam jar or whisking in a small bowl) until well mixed, and pour over the veg in the mixing bowl. Use your hands to lift and toss it all until everything is beautifully coated.

Transfer to a large serving bowl. Peel the eggs, which should now be marbled with soy sauce, slice each one in half and add to the bowl. Top with the crispy shallots, and sprinkle with radish shoots and chilli flakes – and toasted sesame seeds if you like.

 TIP 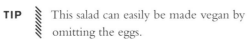 This salad can easily be made vegan by omitting the eggs.

SUMMER

SEARED BEEF & PINEAPPLE RICE WITH CHILLI

When I was backpacking in Vietnam, this simple salad became a firm favourite on balmy summer evenings. I like to serve it in the hollowed-out pineapple shells – which is authentic and delivers some serious wow factor – but you don't have to.

2 small ripe pineapples
240g (8½oz/1¼ cups) jasmine rice
2 tbsp sesame oil
2 red chillies, finely chopped
2 red (bell) peppers, cut into chunks
2 red onions, cut into chunks
2 garlic cloves, finely chopped
100ml (3½fl oz/scant ½ cup)
  pineapple juice

1 tbsp fish sauce
1 tbsp oyster sauce
1 tbsp mirin
300g (10½oz) beef bavette steak
sea salt and freshly ground black pepper

TO SERVE
1 red chilli, sliced
small handful of coriander (cilantro) leaves

On a large chopping board, very carefully cut each pineapple in half lengthways, so both halves have some leaves at the top. Then, with a sharp knife and a spoon work from the top to the bottom of the pineapple, cutting the flesh away from the skin. Repeat with the other pineapple halves and when you have four shells, put them to one side to serve everything in later. Remove the core from the pineapple flesh and slice it into wedges, then into bite-size chunks. Set aside.

Cook the jasmine rice according to the packet instructions. Once cooked, drain and set aside.

Heat 1 tablespoon of the oil in a wok over a medium–high heat and add the chilli, red pepper and onion. Stir-fry for 5 minutes until it becomes aromatic and the onion starts to soften. Add the garlic and cook for 30 seconds. Add the pineapple juice and simmer until it reduces by about half. Next, add the fish sauce, oyster sauce and mirin, and cook for another 2 minutes. Add the pineapple chunks and jasmine rice and stir into the sauce. Remove from the heat.

Rub the remaining oil all over the steak and season lightly. Heat a frying pan (skillet) and then add the steak. Cook for 2 minutes on each side – this will give you medium rare – bavette gets tougher the longer you cook it so do be mindful. Once it is seared all over, transfer to a board and leave to rest for 5 minutes.

Heap the pineapple rice into the pineapple shells. Slice the steak into 5-mm (¼-in) slices and lay them on top of the rice. Sprinkle over chilli slices and coriander leaves before serving.

TOMATO & BURRATA WITH BASIL & WALNUT PESTO (V)

Burrata is mozzarella's creamier, more decadent cousin but a good-quality buffalo mozzarella would work just as well here. Fresh tomatoes taste like sunshine; flashing some of them through the oven develops their flavour, adding another level of interest to this mouthwatering salad.

400g (14oz) on-the-vine cherry tomatoes
1 tsp dried oregano
4 heirloom tomatoes, sliced into rounds
2 beef (beefsteak) tomatoes, sliced
 into rounds
100g (3½oz) baby-leaf salad leaves
1 tbsp extra virgin olive oil
2 burrata (about 400g/14oz)
sea salt and freshly ground black pepper

FOR THE PESTO
50g (1¾oz/2 cups) basil leaves

50g (1¾oz/½ cup) walnuts, toasted and
 crumbled
1 garlic clove, finely grated (minced)
30g (1oz) Parmesan cheese, grated
 (shredded)
120ml (4fl oz/½ cup) olive oil
sea salt and freshly ground black pepper
vegetable oil, for frying

TO SERVE
10g (⅓oz) Parmesan cheese shavings
40g (1½oz/generous ⅓ cup) walnuts,
 toasted

Preheat the oven to 190°C/170°C fan/375°F/gas mark 5 and line a large roasting tin with non-stick baking parchment.

Lay the cherry tomatoes out in the tray. Season with a little salt and pepper and the dried oregano. Pop into the oven for 12–14 minutes, until they just start to burst their skins. While these are roasting, lay the slices of heirloom and beef tomato out on a serving platter.

Put the leaves in a mixing bowl, drizzle over the extra virgin olive oil and toss to coat the leaves. Scrunch them together in your hands to shape them into a big ball, then put them in a mound in the middle of the platter and top with the two burrata.

To make the walnut pesto, first set aside 15 of the basil leaves for later. Roughly tear the remaining leaves into a food processor and add the walnuts and garlic. Blitz to a coarse paste. Add the Parmesan and olive oil and blitz again until you have a lovely pesto. If you'd like it a little thinner, add a splash more oil. Season to taste and mix once more. Set aside. *Continued overleaf*

ROAST TOMATO & BURRATA SALAD WITH
BASIL & WALNUT PESTO

Cover the base of a frying pan (skillet) with a thin layer of vegetable oil, and set over a low heat. Add the 15 reserved basil leaves in two batches. They will sizzle and pop and may spit if the oil is too hot, so do be careful not to burn yourself. The leaves take less than 30 seconds to get crispy and, when you remove them from the oil, they go like stained glass! Really very beautiful and a perfect topper to this salad. When they are ready, carefully lift them out of the oil and leave to drain on some paper towel.

Gently press down in the centre of the burrata to break them open, releasing and exposing their creamy insides. Lay the lightly roasted vine tomatoes around the burrata. Dollop the pesto randomly all over, top with the Parmesan shavings, crumble over the walnuts and finally add the crispy basil leaves.

GREEN BEAN SALAD WITH CHIPOTLE HONEY GLAZE (V)

This is a great, super-quick salad perfect for BBQ season with its spicy chipotle glaze. You can mix up as many types of bean as you like, but this is my favourite combination as you get a lovely variety of tastes and textures. It's sweet, smoky, spicy and utterly divine.

1 tbsp olive oil
½ tsp yellow mustard seeds
½ tsp black mustard seeds
2 garlic cloves, thinly sliced
150g (5½oz) green beans
150g (5½oz) mangetout (snow peas)
150g (5½oz) sugar snap peas
200g (7oz) stringless helda beans or runner
  (Kentucky green) beans, cut into 3-cm
  (1-in) slices
3 tbsp water

200g (7oz) feta, crumbled

FOR THE GLAZE
4 tbsp chipotle paste
2 tbsp runny honey
2 tbsp maple syrup
1 tbsp Dijon mustard
1 tbsp cider vinegar

TO SERVE
50g (1¾oz/½ cup) flaked (slivered) almonds,
  toasted
1 tsp chipotle chilli flakes

Place all the ingredients for the glaze into a small saucepan over a medium heat. Slowly bring to the boil, then lower the heat to a simmer and cook until it becomes thicker and stickier and reduced by about a third. This should take approximately 10 minutes.

While the sauce is reducing, heat a wok over a medium–high heat with the olive oil and add the mustard seeds. They will quickly start to sizzle and pop and when they do, add the garlic and the prepped beans and peas. Add the water, so the veg part-steams in the wok. Keep stirring everything as you don't want anything to take on any colour or the garlic to burn. After about 6–8 minutes, the beans should be cooked just enough – you want them to still be crisp and crunchy.

Add the chipotle glaze to the wok and toss, so the beans get coated, then cook for another minute or two. Transfer the beans to a large serving dish and scatter over the feta. Top with the almonds and chipotle chilli.

pictured on page 63 (top)

TIP This salad can easily be made vegan by omitting the feta and honey.

OCTOPUS SALAD WITH SOURDOUGH MELBA TOASTS

This was a salad I first had on holiday in Portugal where everything is cooked simply to let the ingredients shine. Make this in advance and stash in the fridge to chill and marinate until you are ready to eat. This is all about the fresh citrus, chilli heat and very tender octopus, albeit Cornish in this case!

2 Cornish octopuses, fresh (about 1.5kg/3lb 5oz in total)
1 tbsp peppercorns
2 bay leaves
2 white onions, finely chopped
200g (7oz) radish, thinly sliced on a mandolin
3 garlic cloves, very finely chopped

2 tsp flat-leaf parsley leaves, roughly chopped
6 tbsp extra virgin olive oil
3 lemons, juice, plus the zest of 1
2 red chillies, finely chopped
1 round butterhead lettuce, leaves picked
500g (1lb 2oz) sourdough bread, cut into 5-mm (¼-in) slices

Place the octopuses in a deep saucepan or stock pot. Pour in cold water to cover by 5cm (2in). Add the peppercorns and bay leaves. Place over a low heat and slowly bring to simmering point: you want to poach the octopuses gently, not boil them. Simmer for 40 minutes (or 1 hour for a single large Spanish octopus). When the octopuses are ready, you will be able easily to pierce the top of the legs with a skewer. If there is any resistance, cook for another 10 minutes and test again. Carefully drain, discard the aromatics and rinse under cold water to stop them cooking further.

Put the rest of the salad ingredients into a large mixing bowl, except for the lettuce. Slice all the legs off the octopuses, and discard the heads. Slice the thicker parts of the tentacles into bite-size pieces, and leave some of the thinner curls whole.

Add the sliced octopus to the bowl and mix well to coat in the lemon juice, oil and seasonings. You can now store this for up to 2 days before eating – the flavours will just keep developing.

To make the melba toasts, preheat your grill (broiler) and lay out the thin slices of sourdough. Turn frequently to try and stop them going curly under the heat, until they are a lovely light golden colour on both sides. Stack these crispy little toasts down one end of a platter, or on a separate plate. Spread the butterhead lettuce leaves over the base of your platter and top the lettuce with the octopus salad.

pictured on page 62 (top)

BLACK BEAN, BROAD BEAN & PRAWN TOSTADAS

This is just out-of-this-world crazy tasty. It's a Mexican-inspired salad that tastes like summer and deserves to be enjoyed with friends and eaten greedily. It's messy and fun – just don't forget lots of napkins and a finger bowl or two!

FEEDS 6

300g (10½oz) baby broad (fava) beans
3 tbsp olive oil
2 tsp smoked paprika
1 tsp chilli powder
1 tsp garlic powder
1 tsp dried oregano
1 tsp chipotle chilli flakes (crushed chilli)
600g (1lb 5oz) large raw prawns (shrimp), deveined
400g (14oz) can black beans, drained and rinsed
300g (10½oz/1½ cups) sweetcorn (whole kernel corn)
300g (10½oz) ripe tomatoes, deseeded and chopped
1 red (bell) pepper, diced
1 green (bell) pepper, diced

2 echalion (banana) shallots, finely chopped
2 avocados
juice of 2 limes
1 tbsp coriander (cilantro) leaves, roughly chopped

FOR THE TOSTADAS
vegetable oil, for frying
6 flour tortillas, cut into quarters
sea salt

TO SERVE
4–6 large raw prawns (shrimp), shell on
2 limes, cut into wedges
2 jalapeño chillies, thinly sliced
small handful of coriander (cilantro) leaves

Put a pan of water on to boil. Add the broad beans and blanch them for 4 minutes. Drain and run them under cold water to stop them cooking further, and so you can handle them more quickly. Gently squeeze the broad beans so the bright green beans pop out of their tough pale grey skins, catch them in a mixing bowl and keep for later.

Heat a wok over a high heat with the olive oil. Mix all the spices together in a little bowl. When the wok is hot, carefully add the prawns – they will sizzle and spit, so mind out for the splashes. Then quickly tip in all the spices. Give everything a good shake and toss the prawns around until they are well coated and glossy. Keep tossing and shaking the wok, until the prawns are cooked – they will be curled up, pink and opaque – which should take about 5 minutes. Remove from the heat and transfer to a dish along with all the spices and oil as this is your dressing.

Add the black beans to the broad beans in the mixing bowl, along with the sweetcorn, tomatoes, peppers and shallots. Halve the avocados, remove the stone, dice the flesh and add to the bowl. Mix everything together. Add the prawns and the dressing and toss gently to coat. Squeeze over the lime juice and add the coriander and mix again. Set to one side so it can all mingle while you make the tostadas.

Cover the base of a deep sauté pan with 5cm (2in) vegetable oil. Heat the oil to around 180°C/350°F – you can tell it's hot enough when you add a cube of bread and it sizzles. Being very careful, and working in batches, fry the tortilla quarters for approximately 30 seconds, turning them over halfway through cooking. They should go crisp and golden. Remove from the oil and drain on paper towel, sprinkling with a little salt as you go.

Once you have fried all the quarters, you are ready to assemble the salad. Lay out (or stack) the crisp quarters overlapping on the base of a flat platter, leaving a few corners jutting out so there will be something to pick up! Then heap the salad on top, making sure the prawns are evenly distributed.

Pour off all but a teaspoon of the oil from the deep sauté pan into an old jar to dispose of later, and then add the prawns in their shells to the pan set over a medium–high heat. Cook for around 2–3 minutes before you flip them over and repeat. Just before they are done, squeeze the juice of half a lime over them and give the pan a final shake.

Top the salad with these showstoppers, scatter over the jalapeño slices and some extra coriander leaves, and serve with lime wedges.

Spicy, sour and super fresh.

pictured overleaf (right)

BURRITO SALAD WITH BLACK BEANS & QUINOA

Can a burrito be a salad? Of course it can if it's a BIG salad, where salad is the main event, not something sad on the side of your plate. Swapping tortillas with lettuce cups keeps this on the healthier side of naughty. The best of burritos as an almighty salad.

8 chicken thighs, skin on and bone in

1 onion, diced

1 green (bell) pepper, diced

3 garlic cloves, finely chopped

1 tbsp smoked paprika

2 tsp ground cumin

1 tsp cayenne pepper

400g (14oz) can black beans, drained and rinsed

100g (3½oz/½ cup) quinoa, cooked to packet instructions

3 little gem lettuces, leaves separated

2 avocados

6 ripe tomatoes, diced

2 red chillies, chopped

small handful of coriander (cilantro) leaves

120g (4¼oz) mature Cheddar cheese, grated (shredded)

80g (2¾oz/⅓ cup) sour cream

1 lime, zest and juice

TO SERVE
a few splashes of hot pepper sauce

Heat a large frying pan (skillet) that can hold all the thighs at once, or cook in two batches. Place the thighs into the pan, skin side down, to start rendering the fat out. Cook over a medium heat for 6–7 minutes, by which time the skin should be golden and crisp. Flip them over and cook on the other side for 6–7 minutes. Check they are cooked all the way through to the bone before removing from the heat to a chopping board. When cool enough to handle, slice the meat from the bone and set aside.

Add the onion and pepper to the pan and cook for 5 minutes over a gentle heat to soften, but not colour it. Add the garlic and stir for another 30 seconds until it becomes aromatic. Add the spices and mix well. Stir in the cooked chicken thigh meat, then add the black beans and quinoa and cook altogether for a few minutes to heat through, then remove from the heat.

Lay out all the lettuce leaves on a large serving dish and fill the lettuce cups with some of the chicken filling. Halve the avocados, remove the stone and chop the flesh into chunks. Top each lettuce cup with some avocado, diced tomato and chilli, and cover the whole lot with coriander. Add a little of the cheese to each. Mix the sour cream with the lime juice and zest and add a little dollop. All you need to do then is splash over some hot sauce, if you fancy it, and enjoy.

pictured on page 62 (bottom)

PEANUT & STICKY CHILLI CHICKEN RICE NOODLES

This is a great summer salad as you can so easily cook the chicken thighs on the BBQ instead of on the hob. Using chicken thighs gives you a juicier and, I think, more flavoursome final dish. I love this salad and would happily eat it hot or cold.

8 chicken thighs, skinless and bone in
250g (9oz) rice noodles
1 cucumber, peeled, deseeded and sliced
2 carrots, peeled and julienned
150g (5½oz) bean sprouts
100g (3½oz) edamame beans
60g (2¼oz/generous ⅓ cup) peanuts, toasted and roughly chopped

FOR THE MARINADE
3 garlic cloves, roughly chopped
3cm (1in) ginger, peeled and roughly chopped
1 lemongrass stalk, outer layer removed, roughly chopped
2 kaffir lime leaves, roughly chopped
2 tbsp fish sauce

2 tbsp soy sauce
2 tbsp toasted sesame oil
1 tbsp palm sugar
2 tbsp chilli flakes (crushed chilli), less if you don't want it too fiery

FOR THE PEANUT SAUCE
4 tbsp crunchy peanut butter
2 tbsp mirin
2 tbsp soy sauce
juice of 2 limes
2 tsp toasted sesame oil

TO SERVE
small handful of mint leaves
small handful of coriander (cilantro) leaves
lime wedges

Trim any excess fat off the chicken thighs and place them into a shallow dish. Set aside while you make the marinade.

Add all the ingredients for the marinade into a small food processor and blitz until smooth. Tip the marinade over the chicken thighs and turn them all around to coat and cover them. Cover the dish and place in the fridge for a minimum of 1 hour – this could easily be left to marinate overnight if you like a stronger taste.

In the meantime, add all the ingredients for the peanut sauce to a small bowl and whisk well together. Set to one side. *Continued overleaf*

PEANUT & STICKY CHILLI CHICKEN RICE NOODLES

Cook the rice noodles according to the packet instructions (usually simmering or soaking in boiling water for 3 or 4 minutes). Drain into a colander and run under cold water for a few minutes to stop them cooking further.

Remove the chicken from the fridge and heat a large non-stick frying pan (skillet) on a high heat. Place the thighs into the pan (you may need to do this in two batches if you can't fit them all in), along with the marinade. Try not to move the thighs for a few minutes – you want them to start to caramelise and char, and for the sauce to reduce and coat the chicken. After about 5–6 minutes, flip them over to the other side. After another 5 minutes, they should be cooked through, but make sure there is no pink flesh left before removing from the heat. Transfer the thighs to a chopping board and reserve the pan juices.

Tip the noodles into a large mixing bowl. Add the cucumber, carrots, bean sprouts and edamame beans, along with the reserved pan juices. Slice all the meat from the thigh bones and add half to the bowl. Add all the peanut sauce and half of the toasted peanuts, then mix everything together well.

Transfer to a big serving platter. Pile the rest of the sliced thigh meat up high in the middle. Sprinkle over the remaining chopped peanuts and the herbs. Serve with lime wedges.

pictured overleaf (bottom left)

RAW ASIAN PEAR RAINBOW SALAD (VG)

Raw salads are perfect for summer days when you don't want to stand in front of a hot stove or even turn the oven on but you don't want to compromise on flavour. I love mixing fruit into savoury salads – the crisp, perfumed pear and the citrus from the oranges go so well with the more earthy, slightly bitter flavours of the raw veg.

2 Asian pears, peeled, cored and cut into thin slices

3 oranges, segmented

½ red cabbage, shredded

½ white cabbage, shredded

2 red (bell) peppers, thinly sliced

2 large carrots, peeled and julienned

1 cucumber, halved lengthways and thinly sliced

150g (5½oz) sugar snap peas, cut in half lengthways

FOR THE ORANGE GINGER DRESSING

1 orange, zest and juice

3 tbsp light olive oil

1½ tbsp rice wine vinegar

½ echalion (banana) shallot, very finely chopped

2cm (¾in) ginger, peeled and finely grated (minced)

1 garlic clove, finely grated (minced)

sea salt and freshly ground black pepper

TO SERVE

2½ tbsp sesame seeds, toasted

This salad really is as simple as putting all the ingredients into a mixing bowl and adding the dressing.

To make the dressing, simply stir everything together in a small bowl and season to taste. If you like it fruitier, add a little more orange juice; for more of a kick add a little more ginger. Season to taste and then dress the salad.

Heap everything into a serving bowl and cover with toasted sesame seeds.

pictured overleaf (right)

BLACK RICE NOODLES, RADISH & SUGAR SNAPS (VG)

Using black rice noodles makes for a particularly striking salad, where the colours of the radishes and sugar snaps really pop. Watermelon radish is a beautiful Chinese radish with a pale creamy outer skin and a bright pink centre – hence the name. This is a simple salad full of crunch, but the wasabi dressing adds another dimension, bringing some heat to an otherwise cold dish.

250g (9oz) black rice noodles
100g (3½oz) sugar snap peas
200g (7oz) watermelon radishes, thinly
  sliced on a mandolin
200g (7oz) mooli, thinly sliced on a
  mandolin
3 carrots, peeled and julienned

FOR THE DRESSING
2 tbsp soy sauce
1 tbsp wasabi paste
1 tbsp rice wine vinegar
1 tbsp mirin
1 tsp toasted sesame oil

TO SERVE
handful of Japanese baby herb mix
1 tbsp black sesame seeds
pickled ginger
wasabi
soy sauce

Cook the rice noodles according to the packet instructions (usually simmering or soaking in boiling water for 3 or 4 minutes). Add the sugar snaps to the simmering water as well, then drain into a colander and run under cold water for a few minutes to stop them cooking further. Leave to drain while you assemble everything else.

Put both types of radish into a large mixing bowl, along with the julienned carrot. Give the noodles and sugar snaps a last shake, and add to the radish and carrot. Mix everything together well.

Make the wasabi dressing by whisking everything together in a small mixing bowl. The wasabi does have a kick, so start with less if you want to see how strong it is. Pour the dressing over the salad and mix well to coat everything evenly.

Arrange the noodles on a serving plate and top with the salad. Sprinkle with the baby herbs and black sesame seeds, and serve with a heap of pickled ginger and some more wasabi and soy sauce on the side.

pictured on page 68

BBQ CAULIFLOWER TACO SALAD (V)

This is no ordinary salad – this is an absolute feast of a salad. It's big, bold, colourful and great to eat with your hands! Get messy and make every bite a blend of different flavours and textures.

FOR THE BBQ CAULIFLOWER
1 cauliflower
1 tsp ground cumin
1 tsp ground coriander
1 tsp chipotle chilli flakes (crushed chilli)
1 tsp smoked paprika
1 tsp garlic powder
3 tbsp olive oil
juice of 1 lime

FOR THE TACO SALAD
4 flour tortillas
3 tbsp olive oil
2 corn on the cob
4 tomatoes, seeds removed, diced

2 echalion (banana) shallots, finely
  chopped
1 tbsp coriander (cilantro) leaves, roughly
  chopped
2 avocados
juice of 1 lime
½ iceberg lettuce, shredded
100g (3½oz) Cheddar cheese, grated
  (shredded)
40g (1½oz/¼ cup) sour cream
2 jalapeño chillies, sliced

TO SERVE
lime wedges
handful of coriander (cilantro) leaves

Preheat the oven to 180°C/160°C fan/350°F/gas mark 4. Line a roasting tin with baking parchment. Peel the leaves off the cauliflower and use a sharp knife to trim the base so it is flat and can sit upright. Mix together all the spices with the olive oil and lime juice. Use your hands to rub the spice mix all over the outer surface of the cauliflower, then sit the cauliflower in the roasting tin and roast in the oven for 1 hour, turning it round halfway through to make sure it cooks evenly. By the end of the hour, you should be able to slide a skewer into it relatively easily. If you can't, give it another 10 minutes or so.

While the cauliflower is roasting you can make the taco bowl to serve it all in. Line a deep pie dish with non-stick baking paper. Brush both sides of the tortillas with the olive oil and lay them flat in the bottom of the pie dish and up the sides, overlapping them to make a crust of sorts. Press them down firmly onto each other. Put this dish into the oven under the cauliflower and bake until the taco bowl is crisp – about 10–12 minutes – then remove from the oven and leave to cool in the dish.
Continued overleaf

BBQ CAULIFLOWER TACO SALAD

Bring a pan of water to the boil and add the corn cobs. Cook for 8 minutes until tender, then drain. Once the cobs are cool enough to touch, hold them – one at a time – in a mixing bowl and slice the corn off the husks. Add the tomatoes, shallots and coriander to the bowl and mix. Halve the avocados, scoop out the flesh and squeeze lime juice all over it. Add to the bowl and gently mix everything together.

Remove the cauliflower from the oven and leave to cool slightly.

When the taco bowl is cool, you can start filling it. Place some iceberg lettuce up one side, then add the corn and avocado mix, followed by the two cabbages. Break the cauliflower into florets and add to the taco bowl, or serve on the side. Sprinkle over the cheese and spoon on the sour cream. Top with the sliced jalapeños.

Serve with lime wedges and some extra coriander leaves. This is bowl-food, finger-food, big salad, Mexican, BBQ, but ultimately just ever-changing mouthfuls of incredible flavour. Crack the taco, pull it, share it, enjoy it.

TIP This salad can easily be made vegan by omitting the cheese and sour cream.

FLAME-GRILLED OCTOPUS WITH PEPERONATA & BUTTER BEAN SALAD

You don't get more Spanish than octopus. Marry it with peppers and butter beans – two other classic Spanish ingredients – and some smoked paprika, and you have a real centrepiece salad that is delicious hot or cold.

FEEDS 6

1 Spanish octopus, frozen (1.5–2kg/3lb 5oz–4lb 8oz)
1 tbsp peppercorns
3 bay leaves
2 garlic cloves, peeled and bashed
3 tbsp olive oil
1 tbsp smoked paprika
1 tsp garlic powder
sea salt and freshly ground black pepper

FOR THE PEPERONATA
5 tbsp extra virgin olive oil
1 white onion, thinly sliced
3 large red (bell) peppers, cut into chunks

3 large yellow (bell) peppers, cut into chunks
5 garlic cloves, thinly sliced
2 bay leaves
2 tbsp tomato purée (paste)
6 on-the-vine tomatoes, quartered
660g (1lb 7oz) jar of butter (lima) beans, drained and rinsed (about 425g/15oz total drained weight)

TO SERVE
6 slices of sourdough bread
handful of basil leaves
pinch of smoked paprika

Buying your octopus frozen rather than fresh is ideal as the freezing does the tenderising for you. All you need to do is defrost the octopus it in the fridge overnight. When it's defrosted, place the whole octopus into a big, deep saucepan or stock pot. Pour in cold water to cover it by 5cm (2in). Add the peppercorns, bay leaves and garlic cloves, and place on a low heat, and slowly bring to simmering point. You want to poach the octopus gently, not boil it. Once you have reached simmering point, cook for 1 hour. When the octopus is ready, you will be able to get the tip of a skewer into the top of the legs easily – it should slide in and out. If you have any resistance, cook for another 10 minutes and try again. When it's done, carefully drain into a colander, discard the aromatics and rinse under cold water to stop it cooking any more. You can cook the octopus up to two days in advance, as it keeps well if cooled rapidly and chilled in the fridge. *Continued overleaf*

FLAME-GRILLED OCTOPUS WITH PEPERONATA & BUTTER BEAN SALAD

To make the peperonata, put the extra virgin olive oil in another large saucepan over a medium heat. Add the onion and peppers and cook slowly for about 40 minutes. Stir regularly as you want everything to soften and cook without taking on any colour.

Add the garlic, bay leaves and tomato purée. Stir everything well to coat with the purée and cook for 30 seconds to 1 minute, until the garlic just begins to colour.

Add the tomatoes, give it a quick mix, then pop a lid on and cook for another 40 minutes. By this point, everything should be silky soft and smelling amazing. Add the butter beans and cook for another 20 minutes.

When you are ready to eat, slice the legs off the octopus and discard the head. Mix the olive oil, smoked paprika, garlic powder and some seasoning together in a bowl. Add the tentacles and cover them in the oil mixture.

Now it's time to grill (broil) the octopus. If you've got your BBQ going, it will add a whole extra smoky flavour and some gorgeous char marks from the flames. Grill the octopus legs for 2 minutes each side, until they start to blacken. Alternatively, heat a frying pan (skillet) or griddle pan over a high heat. Cook a couple of octopus legs at a time and repeat until they are all cooked.

Toast the sourdough slices, cut them in half and arrange on your platter. Pour in the peperonata and beans, leaving some edges of the toast uncovered to stay crispy while the rest soaks up the juices. Top with the charred octopus tentacles. Sprinkle over the basil leaves and another generous pinch of paprika.

TIP This salad can easily be made vegan by omitting the octopus. The peperonata is truly delicious even on its own.

GRIDDLED PEACHES WITH WATERCRESS & RICOTTA SALATA (V)

This is a taste of Italian summer. White peaches are usually a little sweeter, but you can use regular peaches or a combination of the two depending on what you can get hold of. Try and find fruits that have been grown as close to home as you can – that means more time ripening in the sun rather than on the shelves, so you get lots more yummy flavour. Ricotta salata is ricotta that has been pressed, salted and dried, so it's hard and salty. If you can't find it, use the same amount of feta instead or half the quantity of pecorino.

6 peaches (white, yellow or a mix)
300g (10½oz) Tenderstem broccoli
80g (2¾oz) watercress, tough stalks
  discarded
4 heirloom tomatoes, sliced into rounds

1 red onion, very thinly sliced
200g (7oz) ricotta salata, crumbled
2 tbsp extra virgin olive oil
freshly ground black pepper

Place a griddle pan over a medium–high heat. Halve the peaches, remove the stones and cut each half into three wedges. When the griddle is hot, add the peaches, cut side down.

Try not to move the peaches for 2 minutes – you want them to start to caramelise where they are in contact with the griddle. Once they have some lovely colour on one side, flip them over and cook for another 2 minutes. Then remove from the pan and set aside.

Bring a pan of water to the boil, with a steamer basket and lid. When it is boiling, add the broccoli and steam for around 4 minutes until al dente. Drain and leave to cool slightly.

Lay out the watercress on a large platter and top with the tomatoes and red onion. Add the broccoli and peaches. Crumble over the ricotta salata and drizzle with a good glug of extra virgin olive oil.

Season with pepper to taste, and serve immediately.

TIP This salad can easily be made vegan
by omitting the ricotta salata.

CRAB, ASPARAGUS & GRAPEFRUIT

This is one of the lightest, freshest salads in the book and a winner for any seafood lover. The dressing is the key to this – it complements but doesn't overpower the crab, still allowing it to shine through and be the star of the show.

400g (14oz) asparagus spears, trimmed

100g (3½oz) lamb's lettuce

1 cucumber, peeled, deseeded and cut into chunks

1 avocado

2 white grapefruit, segmented, juice reserved

200g (7oz) white crab meat

FOR THE DRESSING

1 red chilli, seeds removed, finely chopped

1 lemongrass stalk, outer leaves removed, finely chopped

2 kaffir lime leaves, finely chopped

juice of 1 lime

2 tbsp grapefruit juice

1 tbsp extra virgin olive oil

sea salt

TO SERVE

small bunch of chives, finely chopped

Bring a large pan of water to the boil with a steamer basket and lid. While you are waiting for it to boil, prep the asparagus – snap the ends off at their natural breaking point and slice thicker stems in half lengthways, leaving thinner ones whole. Steam for 4 minutes until al dente, then remove and run under cold water to stop them cooking any further.

Make the dressing by putting all the ingredients into an clean jam jar and shaking well for a minute or so.

Add the asparagus to a large mixing bowl along with the lamb's lettuce and cucumber chunks. Add half of the dressing to the bowl and mix everything lightly, then transfer to your serving plate. Halve the avocado, remove the stone and slice it. Add the avocado, the grapefruit segments and the crab meat to the serving plate.

Drizzle over the rest of the dressing and sprinkle with the chives.

FATTOUSH SALAD WITH HEIRLOOM TOMATOES (VG)

This Middle-Eastern salad makes the very most of some key summer produce. Crisp and simple, its flavours go so well with everything that it is usually served with most Middle Eastern meals. But I think it makes a great BIG salad – it has everything you need.

2 large flatbreads
1 tbsp olive oil
2 romaine lettuces, sliced
600g (1lb 5oz) ripe heirloom tomatoes,
   cut into irregular bite-size chunks
   (if you can't get heirloom then just mix
   up what you can)
6 small cucumbers, cut into irregular
   bite-size chunks
200g (7oz) radishes, quartered
1 bunch of spring onions (scallions), sliced
1 green (bell) pepper, diced
small handful flat-leaf parsley leaves
small handful of mint leaves

FOR THE DRESSING
2 tbsp extra virgin olive oil
juice of 1 lemon
1 tbsp pomegranate molasses
1 tbsp sumac
1 tsp dried oregano
1 garlic clove, finely grated (minced)
sea salt and freshly ground black pepper

TO SERVE
pomegranate molasses
sumac

Preheat the oven to 170°C/150°C fan/325°F/gas mark 3 and line two baking sheets with baking parchment. Brush the two flatbreads with the oil on both sides and then pop them into the oven to go crisp and golden, which should take about 14–16 minutes. Turn them once halfway through cooking. Remove from the oven and leave to cool, then break them into chunks ready to go into the salad.

Put the lettuce, tomatoes and cucumbers into a large mixing bowl. Add the radishes, spring onions and green pepper. Mix everything together.

Add all the ingredients for the dressing to an old jar, season to taste, and shake well to blend. Only add this to the salad once you are ready to eat or the bread will get too soft.

Reserve a few fresh herb leaves to decorate the top of the salad, and roughly chop the rest. When you are ready to eat, add these and the dressing to the salad and mix well. Finally, stir through the crispy flatbread pieces and pour out onto a big serving plate. Sprinkle with the reserved herbs and serve immediately, with a little more pomegranate molasses and sumac on the side.

END OF SUMMER TOMATO SALAD WITH ROASTED FETA & PINE NUTS (V)

Tomatoes really come into their own towards the end of summer when they've soaked up all the sun's rays. Their sweet flesh goes so well with the baked salty feta and basil. It's guaranteed to keep those end-of-summer blues at bay for a little bit longer.

small handful of fresh oregano leaves

2 tbsp extra virgin olive oil

zest of 1 lemon

2 tbsp chilli flakes (crushed chilli)

2 x 200-g (7-oz) packets of feta

90g (3oz) rocket (arugula)

400g (14oz) mixed tomatoes, cut into rounds

1 echalion (banana) shallot, cut into very thin rings

180g (6¼oz/1¼ cups) mixed olives, pitted

small handful of basil leaves

40g (1½oz/¼ cup) pine nuts, toasted

TO SERVE

3 tbsp extra virgin olive oil

1 tbsp balsamic vinegar

freshly ground black pepper

Preheat the oven to 180°C/160°C fan/350°F/gas mark 4 and take a large sheet of baking parchment and lay it on your kitchen counter. Put half the oregano, olive oil, lemon zest and chilli flakes in the middle of the paper – roughly the size of the two blocks of feta. Stir it altogether and lay the feta on top next to each other. Add the rest of the oregano, oil, lemon zest and chilli flakes on top and then carefully lift up the top and bottom edges of the paper. Bring them together up in the air above the feta and start to fold them down in small folds, over and over, until you nearly reach the feta. Then, fold the two open ends underneath the feta so you have a closed parcel. Slide it onto a baking sheet and pop it in the preheated oven for 30 minutes.

In the meantime, arrange the rocket on a serving platter, then layer up the rounds of tomato and shallot rings. Sprinkle over the olives, basil leaves and pine nuts.

Remove the feta from the oven and crumble one block over the platter and leave the other whole to make a centrepiece statement. Drizzle over the olive oil and balsamic vinegar and top with a twist of black pepper.

AUTUMN

HONEY CORNBREAD, SMOKY PEPPER & SWEETCORN

Cornbread is such a treat – it is best served warm from the oven, but still delicious cold. This makes more cornbread than you'll need for the salad, but it will keep for a good few days – if it lasts that long!

FOR THE CORNBREAD
4 eggs, at room temperature
470ml (16fl oz/scant 2 cups) whole milk
40g (1½oz/scant 3 tbsp) unsalted butter, melted and cooled
300g (10½oz/1¾ cups) fine ground polenta (cornmeal)
300g (10½oz/generous 2 cups) plain (all-purpose) flour
75g (2¾oz/scant ⅓ cup) light brown soft sugar
1 tsp baking powder
1 tbsp sea salt
60g (2¼oz/¼ cup) lard

FOR THE PEPPER AND SWEETCORN SALAD
3 tbsp olive oil
2 red onions, sliced
460g (1lb) jar of roasted red (bell) peppers, drained and torn into strips
300g (10½oz/1½ cups) sweetcorn (whole-kernel corn)
1 tbsp smoked paprika
1 tsp garlic powder
1 tsp ground cumin
150g (5½oz) watercress

FOR THE SOAKING SAUCE
75g (2¾oz/⅓ cup) unsalted butter
75g (2¾oz/¼ cup) good-quality runny honey

Preheat the oven to 190°C/170°C fan/375°F/gas mark 5.

First make the cornbread: in a large jug, whisk together the wet ingredients (eggs, milk and melted butter). Then mix all the dry ingredients (polenta, flour, sugar, baking powder and salt) in a large mixing bowl. Make a well in the dry ingredients and start to whisk in the wet ingredients until it is all combined into a thick batter.

Heat a cast-iron or ovenproof frying pan (skillet) over a medium–high heat and add the lard. When it is melted and hot, pour in the batter – you want it to sizzle when the batter hits. This starts the cooking process but you don't need to stir it as it will find its own level. *Continued overleaf*

HONEY CORNBREAD, SMOKY PEPPER & SWEETCORN

Turn the heat off and put the frying pan into the preheated oven.
Bake for about 30 minutes until beautifully golden and risen. As with
a cake, you'll know it's done if it starts to pull away from the edges of
the pan and a skewer inserted into the middle comes out clean. If it's
still wet in the middle, bake for another 5 minutes and check again.
Repeat if necessary.

While the cornbread is baking you can assemble the rest of the salad. Heat
a wok on high and add the oil. Add the onions, peppers, sweetcorn and
the spices and mix everything together well. Cook for about 10 minutes –
you want the veg to catch some colour and get a little charred; this creates
the lovely smoky taste that suits peppers so well.

Put the watercress in a large serving bowl, add the pepper mix and toss
everything together.

Make the soaking sauce for the cornbread by heating the butter and
honey in a saucepan over a low heat. When the cornbread is done,
remove the pan from the oven and pour the sauce over it. Slice half of
the cornbread and place on your serving board (you can keep the rest for
another day) and serve alongside the smoky pepper salad. Yummy.

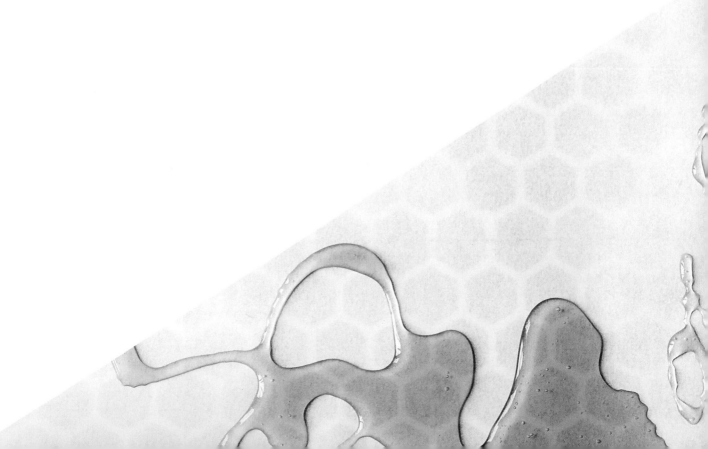

PANZANELLA

This classic Italian salad is brilliant for using up leftovers, everything from slightly soft peppers to over-ripe tomatoes and stale bread. It is very forgiving if you want to omit an ingredient or sub something else in, though be sure to retain the tomatoes and bread.

1 red onion, thinly sliced
pinch of sugar
pinch of sea salt
2 red (bell) peppers
1 yellow (bell) pepper
600g (1lb 5oz) ripe mixed tomatoes,
  roughly chopped
½ cucumber, peeled and cut into chunks
250g (9oz) stale sourdough bread, cut into
  2-cm (¾-in) pieces
3 fresh anchovy fillets (if you
  can't get fresh anchovies use
  marinated instead), finely chopped

2 garlic cloves, finely grated (minced)
2 tbsp capers, rinsed and finely chopped
80g (2¾oz) black olives, pitted and halved
5 tbsp extra virgin olive oil
2 tbsp red wine vinegar
2 tsp basil leaves, roughly
  chopped
sea salt and freshly ground black pepper

TO SERVE
handful of basil leaves

Preheat the oven to its hottest setting and line a roasting tin with foil.

Place the sliced onion into a small bowl and add the pinch of sugar and salt. Toss to coat and set aside.

Lay the peppers in the lined tray and roast in the oven for 30 minutes, turning halfway through. When the skins are black all over, remove from the oven, carefully transfer to a freezer bag and seal it to trap the steam. Leave to one side until they are cool enough to handle.

Place the tomatoes in a large mixing bowl. Give them a gentle squeeze with your hands to break them down slightly, so they release some juices. Add the cucumber, bread, chopped anchovies, garlic, capers, olives, oil and vinegar. Rinse the onions and add them, too.

By now the peppers should be cool enough to handle. Peel off the charred skins, pull them open and remove the seeds. Tear them into strips and add them to the tomato and bread mix. Stir together then leave to stand for 30 minutes minimum, ideally 1 hour, so the bread has time to soak up the juices.

When you're ready to serve, add the chopped basil and give it one last stir. Transfer everything to a shallow serving platter that will hold all the juices, garnish with some basil leaves and season well.

CHILLI SALMON, CARROT, KALE & BUCKWHEAT

Buckwheat is actually not wheat at all, so don't be fooled. It is, in fact, a nutrient-rich, gluten-free seed that is high in protein and fibre, and when combined with the chilli salmon in this salad makes for a really satisfying dish.

500g (1lb 2oz) salmon fillet

3 tbsp sweet chilli sauce

150g (5½oz/scant 1 cup) buckwheat

1 tbsp olive oil

1 red onion, sliced

3 garlic cloves, finely grated (minced)

3 thyme sprigs

300g (10½oz) baby carrots, washed, large
  ones cut in half lengthways

400g (14oz) kale, tough stalks removed

juice of 2 oranges

sea salt and freshly ground black pepper

Preheat the oven to 180°C/160°C fan/350°F/gas mark 4.

Line a small baking sheet with foil and lay the salmon on top. Cover with the sweet chilli sauce and rub all over the top and sides. Bake in the oven for 10 minutes. Meanwhile, cook the buckwheat according to the packet instructions (usually simmering for 8–10 minutes), until al dente. Then drain and leave to steam dry.

Once the salmon has had 10 minutes in the oven, remove and set aside. Put your grill (broiler) on a high heat.

Heat the oil in a large sauté pan and add the onion. Cook for 5 minutes until it starts to soften. Add the garlic and toss it through the onion for 30 seconds until it becomes aromatic. Add the thyme sprigs and carrots and keep cooking, shaking the pan regularly, for 10 minutes.

Baste the salmon with any chilli sauce that has run off and then place it under the hot grill for about 8 minutes until caramelised on top.

Add the kale and the orange juice to the carrots in the sauté pan and cook until the orange juice reduces and coats the veg (there will be no actual thin liquid left) and the kale has just started to wilt – roughly 5 minutes. Add the buckwheat and toss everything together. Season with salt and pepper and transfer to a platter.

pictured on page 97 (centre)

FRIED PLANTAIN, SPICY BEANS & YOGURT DRESSING (V)

This is a really quick salad to rustle up for a hungry crowd. Plantain can be tough to peel; if you're having trouble, top and tail them and cut through the ridges on the skin to peel it off in pieces. You want very ripe ones, so choose ones with blackened skin.

2 tbsp olive oil

20g (¾oz/1½ tbsp) butter

3 ripe plantain, peeled and cut into 1-cm (⅓-inch) slices

400g (14oz) can pinto beans, drained

400g (14oz) can kidney beans, drained

1 avocado

1 red (bell) pepper, chopped

1 green (bell) pepper, chopped

1 red onion, chopped

100g (3½oz) cherry tomatoes, halved

100g (3½oz/½ cup) sweetcorn (whole-kernel corn)

2 tsp coriander (cilantro) leaves, roughly chopped

100g (3½oz) baby leaf spinach

3 chillies, thinly sliced (any kind you like)

FOR THE DRESSING

3 tbsp natural (plain) yogurt

2 tbsp olive oil

1 lime, zest and juice

2 tsp coriander (cilantro) leaves, roughly chopped

1 garlic clove, roughly chopped

½ tsp ground cumin

½ tsp cayenne pepper

pinch of sea salt

TO SERVE

2 tsp chilli flakes (crushed chilli) (optional)

Heat a frying pan (skillet) on a medium heat with the olive oil and butter, and when the butter starts to smell a little nutty, add the plantain in a single layer (you may need to do this in two batches). Leave them to froth and foam for about 3 minutes, give the pan a shake to dislodge them and then flip them over and cook them on the other side. You want them to be golden brown with lovely caramelised edges. Once they're cooked, transfer to some paper towel to drain off any excess oil and butter.

While the plantain is frying, put the pinto and kidney beans into a large mixing bowl. Halve the avocado, remove the stone, chop the flesh and add it to the bowl, along with the peppers, onion, tomatoes, sweetcorn and coriander. Mix everything together well.

Place all the ingredients for the dressing into a food processor and blitz. Add half to the mixing bowl and toss everything together. Lay the spinach leaves on a serving dish and top with the bean mix. Place the slices of fried plantain on top. Finish the dish with the sliced chillies and the chilli flakes, if using.

pictured overleaf (top centre)

BALSAMIC FIG & BAKED GOAT'S CHEESE SALAD WITH HEMP HEARTS (V)

This is such a delicious autumnal salad – and warming too. The hemp hearts add a lovely nutty flavour to the jammy, sticky sweetness of the baked figs and salty goat's cheese.

10 fresh purple figs, quartered or halved depending on their size
2½ tbsp balsamic vinegar
2 tbsp honey
small handful of thyme sprigs
100g (3½oz) goat's cheese, crumbled
2 tbsp extra virgin olive oil

20g (¾oz) shelled hemp seeds (hemp hearts)
50g (1¾oz) rocket (arugula)
50g (1¾oz) baby leaf kale
zest of 1 lemon
sea salt and freshly ground black pepper

Preheat the oven to 200°C/180°C fan/400°F/gas mark 6.

Find a roasting dish that will fit all the figs in one layer and arrange them inside. Drizzle over the balsamic vinegar and honey. Tuck the thyme sprigs in and around everything and pop the dish into the oven to roast for 12–15 minutes, until the honey is bubbling and the figs are softening and browning slightly around the edges.

Remove the dish from the oven and add the crumbled goat's cheese and the oil. Return to the oven for another 10 minutes.

Place the hemp seeds onto a lipped baking sheet and pop into the oven on a shelf under the figs and toast for 7 minutes. Put to one side until you need them.

When the figs are cooked, take the dish out of the oven and remove the figs and cheese. Toss the salad leaves in the sticky juices and then arrange on your serving plate. Place the figs and cheese on top of the salad leaves.

Scatter the toasted hemp seeds over the top and grate over the lemon zest. Season to taste and serve immediately.

pictured on page 96

BEJEWELLED CAULIFLOWER WITH ALMONDS & ZA'ATAR (V)

By lightly roasting the cauliflower, you bring out the most delicious nutty flavours, giving another dimension to its earthy nature. Mix in all the other fresh veg and fruit and it truly looks bejewelled.

FEEDS 6

1 cauliflower

6 large eggs, at room temperature

2 carrots, peeled and julienned

2 large oranges, segmented

50g (1¾oz/scant ½ cup) sultanas (golden raisins)

100g (3½oz) pomegranate seeds

50g (1¾oz/generous ½ cup) dried cranberries

80g (2¾oz/generous ½ cup) blanched almonds, toasted

40g (1½oz/generous ¼ cup) pistachios, slivered

2 tsp flat-leaf parsley leaves, roughly chopped

2 lemons, zest and juice

4 tbsp extra virgin olive oil

1 tbsp za'atar

sea salt and freshly ground black pepper

Preheat the oven to 180°C/160°C fan/350°F/gas mark 4 and line a large roasting tin (pan) with non-stick baking parchment.

Grate the cauliflower straight into the tin and level it out with your fingertips, then roast for 20 minutes, stirring once halfway through. You want it to just start taking on a little colour, which brings out its nutty flavour, but to still be crunchy.

Bring a large pan of water to the boil and then add the eggs. Boil for 7 minutes, then run them under cold water to stop them cooking further.

Remove the cauliflower from the oven and tip into a large mixing bowl. Add the julienned carrots, orange segments, sultanas, pomegranate seeds, dried cranberries, almonds, pistachios and parsley. Grate in the lemon zest, squeeze over the juice, add the oil and za'atar, and mix everything together. Season to taste, then transfer to a serving dish. Peel and halve the eggs, pop them on top of the salad and garnish with a few parsley leaves.

pictured on page 97 (right)

TIP This salad can easily be made vegan by omitting the eggs.

CHARD, BEETROOT, GOAT'S CHEESE & HAZELNUT (V)

Crisp and crunchy; creamy and tangy; hot and sour – this autumn salad has it all and amazing colours to make sure you're getting lots of different nutrients when the weather turns colder. If you've never tried a totally raw salad, this is a great one to start with.

200g (7oz) Swiss or rainbow chard

150g (5½oz) baby leaf spinach

300g (10½oz) beetroot (beets), purple, yellow, rainbow, whatever you can get, peeled

small handful of flat-leaf parsley leaves

200g (7oz) goat's cheese, crumbled

80g (2¾oz/⅔ cup) hazelnuts, toasted and roughly chopped

FOR THE DRESSING

75g (2¾oz/⅔ cup) ripe raspberries

2 tsp fresh horseradish, peeled and finely grated (minced)

2 tsp golden caster (superfine) sugar

3 tbsp olive oil

2 tbsp red wine vinegar

sea salt and freshly ground black pepper

Start by making the dressing. Put the raspberries into a small bowl and, using the end of a rolling pin, bash them down into a rough paste, releasing their juice. Add the grated horseradish and sugar, and then whisk in the oil and vinegar. Have a little taste and season with some salt and pepper if you like. Leave to one side to let the flavours start to mingle.

Take the chard leaves and layer them up on top of one another on a chopping board. Cut out the thick stems (trying not to lose too much leaf) and keep them for later. Stack all the half leaves on top of each other and cut into 1-cm (⅓-inch) wide slices. Put them in a large mixing bowl. Add the spinach leaves.

Chop off the chard stems where they become wider than a centimetre and discard. Finely slice the rest of the stems and add to the bowl.

Using a mandolin on a very fine setting, slice the beetroot into paper-thin rounds – you really want to be able to see the light coming through them. Add these to the chard along with the parsley leaves. Add half of the salad dressing and toss to mingle everything.

Arrange all the leaves and beetroot on your serving plate. Add the goat's cheese and hazelnuts. Top everything by drizzling over the rest of the dressing.

WARM PEAR, MUSHROOM & RICOTTA SALAD (V)

This is such a lovely autumnal salad, using all the delicious pears that are just coming into season. It actually helps if the pears are still hard, so you don't need to be watching and waiting for them to ripen or trying to plan for the perfect moment.

2 tbsp olive oil
80g (2¾oz/¾ cup) walnuts
40g (1½oz/scant 3 tbsp) unsalted butter
3 lemon thyme sprigs
300g (10½oz) portabellini
  mushrooms, sliced
150g (5½oz) mixed salad leaves
200g (7oz) ricotta

FOR THE DRESSING
30g (1oz/generous ¼ cup) walnuts,
  toasted

30g (1oz) Parmesan cheese, finely grated
  (shredded)
1 garlic clove, finely grated (minced)
3 tbsp walnut oil
2 tbsp cider vinegar
salt and pepper

TO SERVE
Parmesan cheese shavings
¼ nutmeg, freshly grated

Add all the dressing ingredients to a food processor and blitz until it's very smooth. This may take anything up to 5 minutes. Scrape the sides and keep blitzing. Set aside when it's ready.

Heat the oil in a sauté pan over a medium heat, add the walnuts and cook for 5 minutes, flipping them in the pan every now and again, until they give off a nutty aroma and turn a deeper shade of brown.

Cut the pears into quarters, leave the skin on but carefully remove the stalk and the core. Add the butter to the walnut pan and place the pears in, cut side down, as well as the thyme sprigs nestled in and around them. Cook the pears for a couple of minutes, then turn and cook the other cut side in the same way. Finally, flip the pears onto their skin side and cook, basting with the foamy thymey butter, for another few minutes, until they are softened but still hold their shape.

Remove the pears and walnuts from the pan. Turn the heat up and add the mushrooms, flicking the pan to keep them moving. You want them to fry, not steam and become golden brown in the buttery oil. This will take 4–5 minutes.

Throw the salad leaves on a serving plate and add the pears and mushrooms. Dot over the ricotta and dressing. Scatter with the Parmesan and lightly grate over the nutmeg. Tuck in straight away.

ROAST SWEET POTATO & CAVOLO NERO (V)

This salad has all the colours and flavours of autumn. The orange of the sweet potatoes, the deep, dark green of the cavolo nero and the red of the onions. It also happens to be comfort food at its best.

20g (¾oz/1½ tbsp) unsalted butter
4 tbsp olive oil
3 red onions, thinly sliced
1kg (2lb 4oz) sweet potatoes, peeled and
   cut into wedges
1 tsp dried thyme
2 garlic cloves, finely grated (minced)
1 tsp fresh thyme leaves

250g (9oz) chestnut mushrooms, sliced
200g (7oz) cavolo nero, sliced
50g (1¾oz) baby leaf spinach
50g (1¾oz/scant ½ cup) pecans, toasted
sea salt and freshly ground black pepper

TO SERVE
2 tbsp balsamic reduction (page 40)
small handful of thyme leaves

Preheat the oven to 200°C/180°C fan/400°F/gas mark 6. Heat a large frying pan (skillet) over a low heat and add the butter and 2 tablespoons of the oil. When the butter has melted, add the onions. You want to cook these very slowly so that some of the water evaporates and the natural sugars release and caramelise. Stir them every few minutes so they cook evenly, this will take around 25–30 minutes.

While the onions are cooking, put the sweet potato wedges into a large ovenproof dish, along with 1 tablespoon of the oil and the dried thyme, and season well. Shake the dish to coat the potatoes, then place them in the oven and roast for 20–25 minutes, until they are starting to go golden brown and are tender all the way through. Turn them halfway through the cooking time.

When the onions are about half their original volume and golden brown, add the garlic and fresh thyme leaves. Cook for another 5 minutes. Heat another frying pan over a medium heat and add the remaining tablespoon of olive oil. Add the mushrooms and cook on a high heat for 6 minutes, until they have started to turn golden brown. Throw in the cavolo nero and cook for another 2 minutes.

Remove the sweet potatoes from the oven and add the mushrooms and cavolo nero. Stir in the spinach; it will start to wilt in the residual heat. Dot spoonfuls of caramelised onions over the top and crumble over the pecans. Drizzle over the balsamic, season to taste, and finish with fresh thyme leaves.

TIP For a vegan version, use an additional
tablespoon of olive oil instead of butter.

BEETROOT & BLACKBERRY SALAD WITH WALNUT OIL (V)

This has to be one of the most striking-looking salads in this book and perfect to get you into an autumnal frame of mind. Warm beetroot and juicy plump berries contrast with the green leaves – it's deliciously dark and seriously warming.

800g (1lb 12oz) beetroot (beets), mixed colours or all purple, whatever you can get (use the leaves in the salad if you like)
80g (2¾oz) rocket (arugula)
80g (2¾oz) baby leaf spinach
1 small red onion, thinly sliced
70g (2½oz/½ cup) pumpkin seeds
160g (5½oz) goat's cheese

200g (7oz/1¼ cups) blackberries
40g (1½oz/generous ⅓ cup) walnuts

FOR THE DRESSING
3 tbsp walnut oil
1 tbsp balsamic vinegar
1 tbsp red wine vinegar
1 garlic clove, finely grated (minced)
sea salt and freshly ground black pepper

Preheat the oven to 200°C/180°C fan/400°F/gas 6.

Wash the beetroot but don't peel. Rub a little olive oil into each one, wrap in a double layer of foil and place in a roasting tin. Cook in the oven for around 1½ hours, or until tender. They will probably be different sizes so smaller ones will cook more quickly – just remove them from the oven as and when each one is ready, until they are all done.

Allow the beetroot to cool until you can handle them, then top and tail and gently rub the rest of the skin off. This should be really easy, but be warned, it will stain your hands, so I find it useful to wear a pair of disposable gloves. When all the beetroot are peeled, cut them into irregular chunks and put into a large mixing bowl. Add the rocket, spinach, onion and pumpkin seeds, and the beetroot leaves if you are using them.

Put all the ingredients for the dressing into a clean jar with a lid, season to taste, and shake well to blend everything (or just whisk them together in a bowl). Pour half over the salad in the mixing bowl. Mix lightly with your hands and then transfer to a serving dish. Scatter over the goat's cheese and blackberries. Finally, crumble over the walnuts and drizzle over the remaining dressing.

TIP   This salad can easily be made vegan by omitting the goat's cheese.

KOREAN GLASS NOODLES (VG)

This is a delicious Korean-inspired noodle salad, with warm flavours and a spicy kick. If you've not used glass noodles before, you're in for a real treat. They are made from sweet potato and have a firmer texture than rice noodles – perfect for slurping up on chilly nights.

300g (10½oz) sweet potato glass noodles
2 tbsp toasted sesame oil
3cm (1in) ginger, peeled and finely grated (minced)
1 garlic clove, finely grated (minced)
300g (10½oz) shitake mushrooms, sliced
300g (10½oz) choi sum, sliced
4 carrots, peeled and julienned
200g (7oz) spinach

FOR THE DRESSING
2 tbsp gochujang (Korean chilli paste)
1 tbsp doenjang (Korean soybean paste)
1½ tbsp mirin
1½ tbsp fish sauce
1½ tbsp soy sauce
3 tbsp gochugaru (Korean chilli powder)

TO SERVE
4 spring onions (scallions), finely sliced
2½ tbsp sesame seeds, toasted
2 tbsp toasted sesame oil
100g (3½oz) kimchi

Cook the glass noodles according to the packet instructions (usually simmering for around 7 minutes). They should be almost bouncy – not soft! Drain into a colander and run under cold water for a few minutes to stop them cooking further, then leave to dry.

Whisk together the dressing ingredients in a small bowl and put to one side.

Heat the sesame oil in a wok over a medium–high heat until hot. Add the ginger and garlic for 30 seconds, just until it becomes aromatic – you don't want anything to catch and burn so be sure to keep it moving. Add the mushrooms, choi sum and carrots and cook for 2 minutes. Add the spinach and cook just enough for it to start wilting – probably another minute or so. Add the dressing and toss everything together.

Add the glass noodles to the wok and turn off the heat. Mix everything together so it all gets coated in the lovely spicy dressing.

Tip out onto a huge platter and top with the spring onions, toasted sesame seeds and a drizzle of toasted sesame oil. No Korean meal is really complete without kimchi, so serve some on the side. Eat with chopsticks and make sure you're hungry.

FREEKEH & CHICKPEA SALAD WITH PULLED HARISSA LAMB

This for me is the ultimate warm and meaty salad and uses another ancient grain – freekeh, which is young wheat. As this grain is popular in the Middle East, it seems only appropriate to cook it with chickpeas, harissa and lamb. The deep layers of flavour will seduce you…

FEEDS 6

1 lamb shoulder, around 2kg (4lb 8oz)
3 tbsp rose harissa
2 tsp garlic powder
3 onions, sliced
1.5l (6⅓ cups) vegetable stock
700g jar of chickpeas (garbanzo beans), drained and rinsed (about 540g/1lb 3oz total drained weight)

200g (7oz/1¼ cups) freekeh
300g (10½oz) sugar snap peas
small handful of coriander (cilantro) leaves
small handful of flat-leaf parsley leaves
sea salt and freshly ground black pepper

TO SERVE
small handful of coriander (cilantro) leaves

Preheat the oven to 160°C/140°C fan/320°F/gas mark 3.

Place the lamb shoulder onto a chopping board and rub the harissa and garlic powder all over it. Put the sliced onions into a large roasting tin and spread out to cover the base. Sit the lamb on top and pour 500ml (2 cups) of the stock around it to cover the onion. Roast the lamb in the oven for 4 hours. You don't need to do anything to it in this time other than look at it longingly.

When you have 30 minutes' cooking time left on the lamb, add the chickpeas to the roasting tin and coat in the juices.

Add the freekeh to a saucepan and cover with the remaining stock. Bring to the boil and cook according to the packet instructions (usually simmering for 12–15 minutes). Drain off any excess liquid and set aside. *Continued overleaf*

FREEKEH & CHICKPEA SALAD WITH PULLED HARISSA LAMB

Bring a pan of water to the boil and blanch the sugar snaps for 4 minutes, then drain and add them to the freekeh. Add the herbs and a little seasoning.

By now the lamb should be super-tender. Remove it from the oven and transfer to a chopping board. Using two forks, shred the meat.

Pour off any excess lamb fat from the roasting tin and then stir the onions and chickpeas together. Tip the freekeh onto a large serving platter, mound on the chickpeas and onions, and heap the lamb on top. Drizzle over any juices left in the roasting tin. Scatter over some fresh coriander leaves and serve immediately – hopefully to a round of applause.

ROAST SQUASH & BLUE CHEESE WITH FLAXSEED BRITTLE (V)

If you think of autumn you can't help but think of pumpkins and squashes. Combine these with some bitter leaves and creamy, salty blue cheese and you can almost feel yourself sitting by a roaring fire. You can buy psyllium husks at health food stores or online.

1kg (2lb 4oz) mix of pumpkin and squash, peeled (if you like, or not), deseeded and cut into wedges and chunks
3 tbsp olive oil
50g (1¾oz) baby leaf spinach
50g (1¾oz) baby leaf kale
1 red chicory (endive) head, sliced
sea salt and freshly ground black pepper

FOR THE BLUE CHEESE DRESSING
120g (4¼oz) blue cheese, crumbled
75g (2½oz/scant ⅓ cup) sour cream
50ml (1¾oz/scant ¼ cup) buttermilk

2 tbsp mayonnaise
twist of freshly ground black pepper

FOR THE FLAXSEED BRITTLE
40g (1½oz/¼ cup) golden flaxseed
40g (1½oz/¼ cup) brown flaxseed
2 tsp psyllium husks
pinch of sea salt
60ml (2fl oz/¼ cup) water

TO SERVE
40g (1½oz) blue cheese, crumbled

Preheat the oven to 180°C/160°C fan/350°F/gas mark 4. Mix together the flaxseed brittle ingredients in a small bowl and leave to stand for 5 minutes so the psyllium husks and seeds absorb the water. Line a baking sheet with non-stick baking parchment and, using a palette knife, spread out the flaxseed mix as thinly as you can (trying to avoid holes). Bake until it is totally dried out, which should take 30 minutes. Remove from the oven and increase the oven temperature to 210°C/190°C fan/425°F/gas mark 7.

Put the pumpkin and squash chunks into a large roasting tin. Coat them in the oil and season with a little salt and pepper. Pop into the hot oven and roast for 30 minutes, turning them over halfway through. You want the edges to be golden brown and the flesh really tender all the way through.

Meanwhile, make the blue cheese dressing by putting all the ingredients into a small food processor and blitzing until smooth. Set aside until you're ready to use it.

Add the spinach, kale and chicory to the hot pumpkin roasting tin and toss everything together. Turn out onto a large serving platter and drizzle over the dressing. Crack the flaxseed brittle into shards and decorate the top of the salad with them. Finish with an extra crumble of blue cheese.

CHARRED SWEETHEART CABBAGE & TENDERSTEM (V)

I love cabbage. I love all green veg, in fact – I could eat platefuls of the stuff. And this super-simple salad is a recipe that celebrates green things! You'll see what I mean…

1 tbsp olive oil
10g (¼oz/2 tsp) butter, melted
400g (14oz) Tenderstem broccoli
  (broccolini), ends trimmed
1 sweetheart (pointed) cabbage, cut into
  quarters through the root
2 tbsp pumpkin seeds, toasted
1 tbsp poppy seeds
40g (1½oz/¼ cup) pine nuts, toasted
20g (¾oz) Parmesan cheese, shaved
handful of basil leaves

FOR THE DRESSING
1 ripe avocado
4 tbsp mascarpone
2 tbsp natural (plain) yogurt
1 tbsp white wine vinegar
1 lemon, zest and juice
1 garlic clove, finely grated (minced)
2 tsp oregano leaves
small handful of flat-leaf parsley leaves
60ml (2fl oz/¼ cup) extra virgin olive oil
½ nutmeg, freshly grated
sea salt and freshly ground black pepper

First make the dressing – peel the avocado and put the flesh and all the dressing ingredients into a food processor. Season to taste, then blend until super smooth – about 2 minutes. Scrape down the sides and blitz again. Then set aside.

Heat a griddle pan on a high heat. Mix the oil and butter together and lightly brush the broccoli and the cut sides of the cabbage. Place them onto the hot griddle in batches. Use the base of a frying pan (skillet) or a wooden spoon to press down on the broccoli to maximise contact with the griddle pan.

Load a tablespoon with dressing, tip it onto a platter and spread it out with the back of the spoon. As each batch of veg is done, transfer to the platter.

Add a little more dressing and scatter over the seeds, pine nuts, Parmesan shavings and some fresh basil leaves. Serve the rest of the dressing in a bowl so people can help themselves.

BLACK RICE & BAKED AUBERGINE WITH POMEGRANATE MOLASSES (V)

Black rice isn't just a case of style over substance – it is high in fibre and packed with antioxidants, as well as being full of flavour. Cooking the aubergines slowly makes them go very soft and silken, and the sweet-and-sour pomegranate molasses pulls everything together beautifully.

2 large aubergines (eggplants), halved
  lengthways through the stem
3 tbsp olive oil
1 tbsp pomegranate molasses
½ tsp cumin
½ tsp sesame seeds
150g (5½oz/¾ cup) black rice
60g (2¼oz/scant ½ cup) pistachios,
  roughly chopped
100g (3½oz/generous ¾ cup) dried
  cranberries
2 tsp flat-leaf parsley leaves, roughly
  chopped

2 tsp dill leaves, roughly chopped
100g (3½oz) pomegranate seeds
2 tbsp extra virgin olive oil
1 lemon, zest and juice
sea salt and freshly ground black pepper

TO SERVE
100g (3½oz/generous ⅓ cup)
  Greek yogurt
2 tbsp pomegranate molasses
1 tbsp sumac
small handful of dill leaves

Preheat the oven to 200°C/180°C fan/400°F/gas mark 6.

Line a roasting tin with baking parchment and put in the four aubergine halves. Using a sharp knife, slice the flesh in a criss-cross pattern, being careful not to go through the skin. Mix together the olive oil, pomegranate molasses and cumin in a small bowl, then liberally brush half of the mixture over the tops of the aubergine. Reserve the other half for later. Sprinkle over the sesame seeds and place the tin into the oven for 20 minutes.

While the aubergine is baking, cook the rice according to the packet instructions (usually simmering for around 45 minutes). *Continued overleaf*

BLACK RICE & BAKED AUBERGINE SALAD WITH POMEGRANATE MOLASSES

Once the aubergines have had their 20 minutes, they should be starting to soften and relax. Take the tin out the oven and brush them with the remaining oil and molasses mix, working it down into the cuts. Return to the oven and bake for another 40 minutes, reducing the heat to 170°C/150°C fan/325°F/gas mark 3.

When the rice is cooked, drain and leave to steam dry for a few minutes before tipping into a large mixing bowl. Add the pistachios, dried cranberries, parsley, dill and pomegranate seeds. Drizzle over the extra virgin olive oil and lemon juice. Season to taste and then mix everything really well. Transfer to a serving plate.

Remove the aubergine from the oven and lay the aubergine halves on top of the rice. Add spoonfuls of the Greek yogurt around the dish, drizzle over the pomegranate molasses and sprinkle on the sumac. Top with a few dill leaves and the lemon zest and serve immediately.

TIP This salad can easily be made vegan by omitting the yogurt.

WINTER

ORZO WITH ROAST SQUASH, SPINACH & GARLIC (V)

A pasta salad is a wonderful thing and you know that any leftovers will be just as delicious cold the next day. This is simple in its flavours and beautiful because each of the ingredients has equal importance.

800g (1lb 12oz) squash (any type), peeled
  and sliced into 2–3-cm (1-in) chunks
4 tbsp olive oil
300g (10½oz) orzo pasta
200g (7oz) baby leaf spinach
4 confit garlic cloves (see page 30)

20g (¾oz/1½ tbsp) unsalted butter
3 tbsp garlic oil
100g (3½oz/2 cups) fresh breadcrumbs
sea salt and pepper

TO SERVE
Parmesan cheese

Preheat the oven to 200°C/180°C fan/400°F/gas mark 6 and line a baking sheet with baking parchment. Lay out the squash on the sheet, drizzle with two tablespoons of the oil and use your hands to rub it all over the squash. Season well. Pop the tray into the oven and roast for about 45 minutes, or until tender, turning once during the cooking.

Bring a large pan of water to the boil, add the orzo, and cook according to the packet instructions (usually around 7 minutes for al dente). Drain and put it back in the pan, add the spinach and return to a low heat. Stir the spinach through the pasta, along with the remaining two tablespoons of oil, so it starts to wilt. Crush the confit garlic into a purée using the side of a knife, then add it to the pan, along with the butter. Continue to cook until the spinach has softened and the butter and garlic has made a sauce of sorts – a maximum of 2 or 3 minutes. Turn the heat down low to just keep it warm.

Heat a large frying pan (skillet) with the garlic oil over a medium heat and add the breadcrumbs. Fry them until a deep golden brown – for about 5–6 minutes – and then tip out onto paper towel to remove any excess oil.

When the squash is done, add it to the orzo and gently stir to combine. Transfer to a serving dish and top with the garlic breadcrumbs.

Shave a little Parmesan over the top or just let your guests help themselves.

pictured on page 128 (top left)

WILD RICE, ORANGE & HERB SALAD (VG)

Wild rice may take longer to cook than standard white rice but it is worth every second. It is nuttier, has more bite and improves heart health and digestion because it takes longer to break down.

150g (5½oz/scant 1 cup) wild rice

300g (10½oz) baby carrots, washed

2 tbsp olive oil

2 oranges, segmented

1 fennel bulb, finely sliced on a mandolin

60g (2oz/½ cup) flaked (slivered) almonds, toasted

2 tsp mint leaves, roughly chopped

2 tsp flat-leaf parsley leaves, roughly chopped

sea salt and pepper

FOR THE DRESSING

1 orange, zest and juice

2 tbsp extra virgin olive oil

1 tbsp sherry vinegar

sea salt and pepper

Preheat the oven to 200°C/180°C fan/400°F/gas mark 6.

Put the rice in a large saucepan, cover with boiling water and set on a high heat. Return to the boil then place a lid on the pan, turn the heat down and simmer for around 50 minutes, until the grains of rice have popped open.

While the rice is cooking, put the carrots in a roasting tin with some seasoning and the olive oil. Roast them in the preheated oven for around 20 minutes – or until just tender.

Place the orange segments in a large mixing bowl and add the sliced fennel and half the almonds. Add the roasted carrots when they're ready. When the rice is done, drain it, shake it well to remove as much water as you can, and add it to the bowl.

Mix the ingredients for the dressing together in a small bowl or jam jar, season to taste, and pour over everything in the bowl. Add the herbs and gently mix everything together with your hands so as not to break any of the carrots.

Pour everything onto a big platter, sprinkle with the remaining almonds and eat while it is still warm.

pictured on page 129 (top)

BAVETTE STEAK & CHICORY SALAD

This is a hearty winter salad guaranteed to keep the cold at bay. It's a glorious mix of tender meat and potatoes, salty anchovies, crunchy cornichons and tasty herbs – all smothered in a classic mustard vinaigrette. Winter winner!

2 garlic cloves, crushed with the back of a knife

1 echalion (banana) shallot, halved and finely sliced

2 tsp smoked paprika

1 tsp dried thyme

3 tbsp olive oil

500g (1lb 2oz) beef bavette steak

500g (1lb 2oz) new potatoes, washed, larger ones halved

2 white chicory (endive) heads, quartered

2 red chicory (endive) heads, quartered

10 fresh anchovy fillets (if you can't get fresh anchovies use marinated instead)

100g (3½oz/½ cup) sweetcorn (whole-kernel corn)

100g (3½oz) cornichons, chopped

small handful flat-leaf parsley leaves

2 tsp chives, finely chopped

sea salt and freshly ground black pepper

FOR THE DRESSING

3 tbsp extra virgin olive oil

1 tbsp red wine vinegar

1 tbsp Dijon mustard

1 garlic clove, finely grated (minced)

sea salt and freshly ground black pepper

TO SERVE

Dijon mustard

Find a shallow dish that can hold the beef. Add the garlic, shallot, paprika, thyme and olive oil. Mix it together well and then add the steak. Roll it in the mix, cover with plastic wrap and then leave to marinade in the fridge for at least an hour (preferably overnight).

When you are ready to eat, place the potatoes into a large saucepan, cover with cold water and add a pinch of salt. Bring the potatoes to the boil and then keep them on a gentle boil until they are just cooked – about 15 minutes. Drain and leave to steam dry. Chop into bite-size chunks.

Heat a griddle pan on a high heat. Remove the meat from the marinade and put on a plate. Dip the chicory into the marinade, just enough to coat the cut sides. Sear the chicory in the pan for a couple of minutes on each side and then remove the pan from the heat. Transfer the chicory to a chopping board and cut into bite-size chunks, discarding the thick core. Place in a mixing bowl and add the cooked potatoes and anchovy fillets.

Return the griddle to the heat. Give the meat one last roll in the marinade (discarding any of the garlic and shallots) and season well with salt and pepper. Add the steak to the pan and cook for 2 minutes on each side – this will give you medium rare – cook for longer if you like it more well done, but bavette is a great cut for flash-frying and it will get tougher the longer you cook it. Remove the beef from the griddle and leave to rest for 5 minutes on a chopping board.

Add the sweetcorn and cornichons to the mixing bowl, along with the herbs.

Mix the dressing by placing all the ingredients in an clean jam jar, seasoning to taste, and shaking well. Pour over everything in the bowl and mix.

Slice the steak into thin strips going across the grain, which keeps it tender, and add to the bowl. Mix everything together, add any juices that come out the meat and transfer to your serving plate.

Serve with a little pot of extra Dijon mustard on the side.

pictured on page 129 (bottom)

GRIDDLED POUSSINS & MUHAMMARA

This salad is inspired by my travels to the Middle East, where I really fell in love with all the flavours and the passion for using seasonal produce and lots of herbs and spices. This recipe is for half a poussin per person but you could up the quantities to one bird per person and double the quantity of seasoning for the birds.

2 corn-fed poussins
1 tbsp dried oregano
½ tsp grated nutmeg
zest of 1 lemon
20g (¾oz/1½ tbsp) unsalted butter, softened
4 red (bell) peppers
2 garlic cloves, roughly chopped
100g (3½oz/2 cups) fresh breadcrumbs
2 tbsp pomegranate molasses
1 tbsp chilli flakes (crushed chilli)

1 tsp cumin
80g (2¾oz/¾ cup) walnuts
100g (3½oz) rocket (arugula)
1 tbsp extra virgin olive oil
sea salt and pepper

TO SERVE
flatbreads – see page 42
handful of coriander (cilantro) leaves, roughly chopped

Preheat the oven to its hottest setting and line a roasting tin with foil.

The poussins are going to be spatchcocked so they cook a little quicker, and nice and evenly: take one of the poussins and place it on a chopping board, breast side down, legs closest to you. With a very sharp pair of scissors cut up the right-hand side of the spine (staying as close to it as you can). And then cut up the left-hand side to remove it entirely. Turn the bird over while pulling the two cut sides out and round to open up the internal cavity. Press down on the breastbone to flatten it, you may crack it – that's fine, don't be alarmed! Repeat this with the second bird, then place both in a dish that fits into the fridge.

Press the dried oregano, nutmeg and lemon zest into the chunk of soft butter and then rub the butter all over the skin of the birds. Cover with plastic wrap and transfer to the fridge while you start the muhammara. *Continued overleaf*

GRIDDLED POUSSINS & MUHAMMARA

Place the peppers into the prepared roasting tin and pop into the hot oven for 30 minutes, turning halfway through. You want the skins to blacken all over. When they are completely black, remove from the oven and carefully put them into a freezer bag and seal to trap the steam. Leave to one side until they are cool enough to handle. Turn the oven down to 190°C/170°C fan/375°F/gas mark 5.

While the peppers are cooling, heat a large griddle or frying pan (skillet) – something that can go from the hob to the oven. If you don't have something like this, start in a frying pan and transfer to a roasting tin. When the pan is hot, add the poussins skin side down and cook over a medium heat for about 8 minutes, basting occasionally with the buttery juices, until the skin is golden brown. Flip them over so they are cavity side down and cook for another 3 minutes then season them well and pop into the oven for 20 minutes to finish cooking.

When the peppers have cooled, peel off the charred skin, pull them open and remove the seeds. Tear them into strips and put to one side.

Put the garlic into a large pestle and mortar and grind it into a paste. Add the breadcrumbs, one tablespoon of the pomegranate molasses, the chilli and cumin, and work it all together. Once you have a thick-ish paste, start to add the peppers little by little, pounding as you go. If you don't have a large enough mortar, you can, of course, do all this in a food processor – just don't over-blitz as you want everything to still be recognizable, not a purée. Use a spoon to help scrape down the sides of the mortar or bowl, and when you have a nice rough texture with all the peppers combined, stir in the walnuts, bash lightly to break them down and combine.

Spread this muhammara over a platter and top with the rocket. Drizzle over the extra virgin olive oil and the remaining tablespoon of pomegranate molasses. Take the poussins out of the oven and cut them into halves. Pile them in the middle and put a stack of flatbreads on the side. Sprinkle over the coriander leaves and serve immediately.

STICKY AUBERGINE & MUSHROOM SOBA NOODLES

Aubergines are such brilliant vessels for carrying a dish and all its flavours. Their slightly earthy taste goes perfectly with the shiitake mushrooms – another big hitter in terms of health benefits, important for keeping colds at bay in winter.

4 tbsp sesame oil

2 aubergines (eggplants), peeled and diced into rough 2-cm (¾-in) cubes

4 tbsp oyster sauce

1 tbsp soy sauce

1 tbsp fish sauce

1 tbsp mirin

2 red chillies, finely sliced

3 garlic cloves, finely grated (minced)

3cm (1in) ginger, peeled and finely grated (minced)

200g (7oz) shiitake mushrooms, sliced

200g (7oz) purple sprouting broccoli

100g (3½oz) baby leaf spinach

1 bunch spring onions (scallions), finely sliced

200g (7oz) soba noodles

TO SERVE

1 red chilli, thinly sliced

handful of coriander (cilantro) leaves

1 tsp black sesame seeds

Heat a large sauté pan or wok with the sesame oil over a high heat. When it's hot, whoosh it round the pan and add the aubergine. Toss quickly so the oil coats all of the aubergine, not just one side. Reduce the heat to medium and cook, stirring regularly, for 6 minutes until it just starts to soften and brown.

Add the oyster, soy and fish sauces along with the mirin, and stir to coat the aubergine. Reduce the heat to low and add the chilli, garlic and ginger. Mix well and keep cooking over a low heat for another 10 minutes. By this point the aubergine should be soft and coated in the dark, sticky sauce.

Add the mushrooms and broccoli. Cook for 5–6 minutes until they start to soften. Add the spinach and spring onions, and stir through. Leave on the lowest heat for 2 more minutes to allow all the flavours to mingle.

Cook the soba noodles according to the packet instructions (usually simmering for 4 or 5 minutes). Drain well before adding to the aubergine. Flick and shake the pan to incorporate the noodles.

Transfer to a big serving bowl and finish with a final flourish of chilli, coriander leaves and black sesame seeds. Excellent to slurp up with chopsticks.

pictured on page 128 (bottom)

CAULIFLOWER & PUY LENTILS WITH TAHINI & TURMERIC (VG)

Roasting a whole cauliflower makes a real statement. The natural flavour intensifies and the spices enhance it to maximum effect, making it taste almost meaty somehow. The result is a lightly spiced, earthy-tasting warm salad.

FEEDS 6

1 large cauliflower
2 tbsp olive oil
1 tsp turmeric
1 tsp garlic powder
½ tsp ground coriander
½ tsp cumin
150g (5½oz/¾ cup) puy lentils
100g (3½oz) rocket (arugula)
100g (3½oz) pomegranate seeds
50g (1¾oz/⅓ cup) nibbed (slivered)
   pistachios, toasted

1 tbsp olive oil

FOR THE TAHINI AND TURMERIC DRESSING
4 tbsp tahini
4 tbsp olive oil
juice of 2 lemons
6 tbsp water
1 tsp turmeric
½ tsp cayenne pepper
sea salt and freshly ground black pepper

Preheat the oven to 220°C/200°C fan/425°F/gas mark 7.

Peel the leaves off the cauliflower and use a knife to trim the base so it is flat and can stand upright. Make a paste out of the oil and spices and rub this all over the outside of the cauliflower. Stand the cauliflower onto a lipped baking sheet lined with baking parchment. Roast in the oven for 1¼ hours, turning the temperature down to 190°C/170°C fan/375°F/gas mark 5 after the first 20 minutes.

While the cauliflower is roasting, place the puy lentils into a saucepan and cover with cold water. Bring to the boil, then cover with a lid and simmer until they are just cooked, around 25 minutes.

Mix the ingredients for the dressing in a small saucepan, season to taste, and place on a very low heat.

When the lentils are cooked, drain them and tip into a large mixing bowl. Add the rocket, pomegranate seeds, pistachios and olive oil, and stir to just coat everything. Transfer to a serving plate and make a space in the middle for the cauliflower to sit. Take the cauliflower out of the oven and place it in the centre of the plate. Slice a few wedges to expose the pale insides. For a little extra drama, you could insert a steak knife into the top so your guests can carve wedges for themselves. Serve with the warm tahini dressing on the side.

BURNT ORANGE, MACKEREL & KALE WITH BACON

This salad packs a serious punch. As an oily fish, mackerel is a great carrier of other flavours and it goes really well with the salty bacon and the slightly bitter kale. Orange lifts everything and brings a slightly sweet balance to the salad. Ask your fishmonger to butterfly the fish for you.

300g (10½oz) kale, tough stalks removed
250g (9oz) streaky bacon
4 small oranges, halved
4 mackerel, butterflied
250g (9oz/1⅔ cups) cooked puy lentils
2 tsp chives, finely chopped
small handful parsley leaves
sea salt and freshly ground black pepper

FOR THE BACON DRESSING
juice from 2 of the burnt oranges
1 garlic clove, finely grated (minced)
70ml extra virgin olive oil
2 tbsp red wine vinegar
2 tbsp wholegrain mustard
sea salt and freshly ground black pepper

Place the kale into a mixing bowl along with half a teaspoon of crushed sea salt. Massage the salt into the leaves with your hands for a few minutes – the kale will suddenly go much softer. Set to one side.

Heat a large frying pan (skillet) on a medium heat and add the bacon slices. Cook slowly, turning occasionally, until very crisp (6–8 minutes), and then place on paper towel to soak up the excess fat. Keeping the pan on a medium heat, place the orange halves in the hot bacon fat, cut side down, and cook for 4 minutes until charred and caramelised. Set aside while you cook the mackerel. Lightly season the fish on both sides and then lay them into the hot pan, skin side down. Press down gently on the flesh to stop them curling, and cook for 2 minutes. Flip over and cook for another minute.

Place the lentils into a saucepan, add a splash of water and place over a low heat to warm through for a few minutes. Drain and rinse under cold water to stop them cooking any further. Give them a good shake to remove as much water as possible and then tip them in with the kale leaves. Add the herbs.

For the dressing, take four slices of the crispy bacon and crumble them into a food processor, then add all the other ingredients, seasoning to taste. Blitz until you have a smooth(ish) dressing. Add most of the dressing to the mixing bowl and toss gently to combine. Place the kale and lentils onto a platter, top with the mackerel and snap the remaining bacon over the top. Drizzle over the rest of the dressing and place the remaining burnt oranges around to garnish. Serve immediately.

CHICKEN SHAWARMA SALAD WITH PICKLED CHILLIES

This is a big kiss on the lips – to be honest it doesn't have to be a winter salad at all, but anything with a bit of a kick is lovely on a frosty day.

8 chicken thighs, skinless and boneless
2 garlic cloves, finely grated (minced)
1 tsp ground coriander
1 tsp ground cumin
1 tsp smoked paprika
1 tsp garlic powder
½ tsp cayenne
½ tsp ground cardamom
3 tbsp olive oil
juice of 2 lemons
500g (1lb 2oz) ripe tomatoes, sliced
½ iceberg lettuce, shredded

¼ white cabbage, shredded
¼ red cabbage, shredded
200ml (7fl oz/generous ¾ cup) natural (plain) yogurt
2 tsp mint leaves, finely chopped
sea salt

TO SERVE
flatbreads – see page 42
2½ tbsp sriracha hot chilli sauce
40g (1½oz) pickled chillies

Put the chicken thighs into a bowl and add the garlic, all the spices, the olive oil and lemon juice. Mix everything around and cover all the chicken. Leave to marinade for as long as you can – overnight is ideal.

All that's left to do is cook the chicken and assemble the salad. Thread the thighs onto two skewers and heat a griddle pan over a medium–high heat. When it is hot, add the skewers. Cook for 6 minutes, then flip and cook for another 6 minutes, or until cooked through.

While the chicken is cooking, combine the shredded lettuce and cabbages in a mixing bowl, then lay it out on a large platter. In a small bowl, mix together the yogurt and mint, with a pinch of salt. Drop half of the yogurt mix in spoonfuls over the cabbage mix.

When the chicken is cooked, slide it off the skewers, slice into thin strips and place on top of the salad. To finish off, drizzle over the sriracha and top with the pickled chillies. Place the remaining yogurt mix into a bowl on the side. Serve with the flatbreads so you can scoop up salad and chicken and yogurt all at once.

ROMANO PEPPERS STUFFED WITH SPELT SALAD (V)

Spelt is somewhat of a wonder grain, packed full of vitamins and minerals that can boost your immune system, aid circulation, decrease cholesterol and many other things besides.

4 Romano (sweet) peppers, halved lengthways through the stalk, deseeded
3 tbsp olive oil
150g (5½oz/generous ¾ cup) spelt grains
20g (¾oz/1½ tbsp) unsalted butter
1 echalion (banana) shallot, finely chopped
1 leek, halved lengthways, thinly sliced
3 garlic cloves, finely grated (minced)
150g (5½oz) chestnut mushrooms, diced
2 tsp flat-leaf parsley leaves, finely chopped
2 tsp thyme leaves
60g (2¼oz/generous ½ cup) walnuts, toasted and crumbled

40g (1½oz) Parmesan cheese, plus extra to grate (shred)

FOR THE HERB DRESSING
small handful of flat-leaf parsley leaves
small handful of dill leaves
small handful of chives
small handful of basil leaves
80ml (2¾fl oz/⅓ cup) olive oil
2 tbsp cider vinegar
1 tbsp Dijon mustard
2 tbsp water
½ tsp salt

Preheat the oven to 180°C/160°C fan/350°F/gas mark 4. Snugly fit the pepper halves in an ovenproof dish in one layer, cut side up. Brush the insides with 1 tablespoon of the olive oil and set aside.

Place the spelt in a saucepan, cover with cold water, bring to the boil and simmer for 20–22 minutes – you want it still to have a little bite. Meanwhile, blitz all the dressing ingredients in a food processor.

While the spelt is simmering, heat a large frying pan (skillet) with the remaining olive oil and the butter. Add the shallots and leeks and sweat gently for about 10 minutes, stirring occasionally. Once the leek is soft, add the garlic and mushrooms and cook for another 5 minutes.

Drain the spelt well, shaking to remove excess water. Add it to the leeks and mushrooms, along with the herbs and walnuts. Mix everything together gently and then stir in the Parmesan. Fill the pepper halves with the spelt salad and grate a little more Parmesan over the top. Pop them into the hot oven for 20–25 minutes, until the peppers are tender. Remove from the oven and drizzle over some of the dressing, serving the rest on the side. Serve immediately.

pictured on page 145 (top)

SHAVED CAULIFLOWER, KALE & APPLE WITH FENNEL (VG)

Cauliflower is a great source of vitamin C and other nutrients, essential in those darker, colder months. Add to this all the other vegetables, fruits and seeds, providing fibre, proteins, carbs and healthy fats for good measure, and you won't be left feeling hungry.

1 fennel bulb, shaved thinly on a mandolin
zest of 1 orange
100ml (3½fl oz/scant ½ cup) cider vinegar
300ml (10½fl oz/1¼ cups) water
2 tbsp sea salt, plus ½ tsp for the kale
2 tbsp granulated sugar
1 tsp black peppercorns
250g (9oz) kale
1 cauliflower, cut into quarters and shaved
  on a mandolin
2 pink lady apples, cored, halved and sliced
  thinly into half-moon slivers

80g (2¾oz/¾ cup) walnuts, toasted
5 tbsp pumpkin seeds, toasted
5 tbsp sunflower seeds, toasted

FOR THE DRESSING
3 tbsp walnut oil
2 tbsp lemon juice
sea salt and freshly ground black pepper

TO SERVE
small handful of dill leaves

Try to pickle the fennel the night before you want to eat, if you can. You could get away with making it just 4 hours in advance, but the flavours won't have mellowed in the same way.

Put the fennel and orange zest into a clean, airtight container or jar with a lid. Place the cider vinegar and water into a saucepan with the salt, sugar and peppercorns and bring to the boil. When it's boiling and the salt and sugar have dissolved, pour the hot liquid into your container to cover the fennel. Put the lid on and leave to cool to room temperature. Then store in the fridge until you need it.

When you're ready to eat, make the dressing in a clean jam jar – add all the ingredients, season to taste and shake everything together. Place the kale leaves into a mixing bowl along with the half teaspoon of crushed sea salt. Massage the salt into the leaves with your hands for a few minutes – you should find that the kale will suddenly go much softer. Add the shaved cauliflower to the kale, along with the apple slices, nuts and seeds. Pour the dressing over the top and use your hands to gently coat everything.

Lay everything out on a platter and top with some of the pickled fennel. Scatter the dill leaves over everything and serve immediately.

pictured on page 145 (bottom)

PUY LENTIL & BAKED HALLOUMI WITH CRISP CAPERBERRIES (V)

This is such a lovely warming salad, perfect for the start of winter. It's cosy bowl-food at its best with an unconventional caperberry twist!

200g (7oz/1 cup) puy lentils
8 thyme sprigs
2 bay leaves
2 garlic cloves, peeled and lightly bashed
500ml (17fl oz/2 cups) vegetable stock
2 x 250-g (9-oz) packets of
  halloumi cheese
4 tbsp olive oil
1 red onion, chopped
4 ripe tomatoes, seeds removed, diced
50g (1¾oz/⅓ cup) black olives, halved
2 tsp flat-leaf parsley leaves, roughly
  chopped

1 tbsp red wine vinegar
sea salt and freshly ground black pepper

FOR THE CRISP CAPERBERRIES
vegetable oil, for frying
40g (1½oz/⅓ cup) plain
  (all-purpose) flour
pinch of caster (superfine) sugar
80ml (2¾fl oz/⅓ cup) cold fizzy water
60g (2¼oz/scant ½ cup) caperberries,
  drained

Put the puy lentils, four of the thyme sprigs, the bay leaves and garlic into a large saucepan. Cover everything with the stock and place on a medium heat. Bring the stock to the boil, reduce to a simmer and cook the lentils for around 30 minutes or until just tender. Keep an eye on the stock and if the pan starts to look a bit dry, just top up with some boiling water.

Preheat the oven to 180°C/160°C fan/350°F/gas mark 4. Make a little foil tray on a baking sheet and sit the halloumi blocks on it. Top with the remaining four thyme sprigs, a twist or two of black pepper and a tablespoon of the olive oil. Bake for 20 minutes and then turn off the heat and keep it warm until needed.

Once the lentils are cooked, remove all the aromatics. Add the onion, diced tomatoes, olives and parsley. Glug in the remaining olive oil and the red wine vinegar and stir to mix. Taste and season with salt and pepper.

The last thing to do is make the crisp caperberries. In a small sauté pan, add 3cm (1in) of vegetable oil and heat to about 180°C/350°F – you can tell it's hot enough when you toss in a cube of bread and it sizzles.

Make the batter immediately before you want to use it, as the cold fizzy water is integral to getting a light, crispy batter. Put the flour and sugar in a little bowl and whisk in the fizzy water. Don't overbeat or the batter will be anything but light and crisp. Pat the drained caperberries dry with some paper towel and then, holding the caperberry by the stem, drag it through the batter and carefully lower into the oil. Repeat as swiftly and as carefully as you can – you may want to do this in a few batches. When the berries are crisp, lift them out with a slotted spoon and drain on paper towel while you cook the rest.

Remove the halloumi from the oven. Take the puy lentils and spread over the base of a shallow serving dish. Add the sliced halloumi and top with the crisp caperberries (or serve them on the side).

pictured on page 144

ROAST CARROT & SPICED PARSNIP WITH PANEER (V)

This is one of my absolute favourite salads – it is just so yummy! And it's great hot, warm, cold or somewhere in between. Root veg is always going to be best in winter – when it is actually in season – and it's even better after the first couple of frosts.

500g (1lb 2oz) baby carrots, washed and larger ones halved

500g (1lb 2oz) baby parsnips, washed and larger ones halved or quartered

2 bay leaves

4 tbsp olive oil

1 tsp cumin

1 tsp ground coriander

½ tsp nutmeg

½ tsp cinnamon

½ tsp ground ginger

4 tbsp honey

300g (10½oz) paneer, cubed

160g (5½oz) baby leaf spinach

100g (3½oz) raisins or sultanas (golden raisins)

sea salt and pepper

TO SERVE

handful of coriander (cilantro) leaves

1 tbsp nigella seeds

Preheat the oven to 200°C/180°C fan/400°F/gas mark 6.

Put the carrots, parsnips and bay leaves in a large ovenproof roasting dish that you can take to the table. Cover everything in the oil and add the spices before mixing well. Drizzle over the honey, season and place into the hot oven for 20 minutes. Then turn everything over and around, and return to the oven for another 15 minutes. Remove the dish from the oven again and add the paneer cubes. Roast for a final 12 minutes.

When the time is up, take the dish out of the oven and add the raw spinach and raisins. Stir the spinach through all the oil and cooking juices, using the residual heat to wilt it.

Scatter over some coriander leaves and the nigella seeds to garnish before serving.

TIP To make a vegan version of this salad, substitute date syrup for the honey and omit the paneer.

AUBERGINE WITH CRISPY SEAWEED & CHILLI EGGS (V)

This recipe is an explosion of flavour and, once you realise just how easy it is, it will make you question whether you need to order a Chinese takeaway ever again. Aubergines are so versatile and this creates a dish so incredibly moreish that you'll be making it time and time again.

250g (9oz) spring greens, thick stems removed and leaves shredded

vegetable oil, for deep frying

1 tsp sea salt, crushed

1 tsp granulated sugar

750g (1lb 10oz) aubergine (eggplant), cut into 2.5-cm (1-in) chunks

2 tbsp rice flour

1 tbsp sesame oil, plus 1 tsp for the eggs

3cm (1in) ginger, peeled and finely grated (minced)

5 garlic cloves, finely grated (minced)

200ml (7fl oz/generous ¾ cup) black bean sauce

1 tbsp soy sauce

2 tbsp palm sugar

3 tbsp rice wine vinegar

250ml (9fl oz/generous 1 cup) water

4 eggs, at room temperature

1 tsp chilli flakes (crushed chilli)

First you need to turn the shredded greens into crispy seaweed. Bring a large pan of water to the boil, add the greens and blanch for 1 minute. Drain and run under cold water. Shake vigorously to remove as much water as possible before laying out on a clean tea towel. Place a second tea towel on top and pat the greens dry.

Heat the vegetable oil in either a deep fat fryer or a large, deep saucepan that has a lid (fill the pan just under halfway). A thermometer is handy here as you want to get the temperature up to 180°C/350°F. Line a baking sheet with paper towel. Put the salt and sugar into a small bowl and mix.

Check the greens are as dry as possible – the oil will spit anyway but you can minimise it. Holding the lid to the pan in one hand, use your other hand to take a handful of the greens and quickly but carefully drop them into the oil, then immediately put the lid on, covering 90% of the saucepan (so the steam created has somewhere to escape). Leave it on until the oil stops popping and spitting after around 10 seconds. Continue to fry until the greens are crisp – about 30 seconds. Lift them out carefully onto the prepared baking sheet using a slotted spoon and sprinkle over some of the salt and sugar mix. Repeat until all the greens are cooked. *Continued overleaf*

AUBERGINE WITH CRISPY SEAWEED & CHILLI EGGS

Reduce the heat under the oil while you dust the aubergine chunks with the rice flour. Line another baking sheet with paper towel. Bring the oil back to 180°C/350°F. Cook the aubergine in batches until it is a lovely golden brown – roughly 2–3 minutes. Remove from the oil with a slotted spoon and transfer to the prepared baking sheet to absorb the excess oil. Repeat until you have cooked all the aubergine.

Heat a wok with the sesame oil over a medium–high heat, add the ginger and garlic and cook, keeping it moving so nothing catches and burns, for 30 seconds. Add the black bean sauce, soy sauce, palm sugar, rice wine vinegar and water. Give it all a little stir and bring it up to the boil before reducing to a simmer and adding the deep-fried aubergine.

Stir gently until the aubergine is coated with the sauce, then cook for around 20 minutes, stirring regularly. By this time, the aubergine should have softened and be coated in a thick, sticky, shiny sauce. The aubergine will be very tender but try not to break it up too much when you stir. Then turn the heat down to as low as you can to just keep it warm, and heat a frying pan (skillet) on a high heat with 1 teaspoon of sesame oil.

Crack in the four eggs and sprinkle the yolks with a few chilli flakes. Once the eggs are crispy round the edges and the yolks cooked to your liking, turn off the heat.

Spoon the aubergine onto a large plate and top with the four fried eggs. Sprinkle over the crispy seaweed and serve immediately.

 TIP 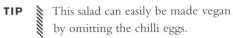 This salad can easily be made vegan by omitting the chilli eggs.

SHREDDED DUCK, ROAST ROOT VEG, KALE & SPICED ORANGE

A roast duck is a real treat and this recipe makes it the star of the show. Duck is often seen as a rather fatty option but by slow-cooking it, you render out a lot of the fat and the meat becomes amazingly tender and stays very moist.

2 tsp Chinese five spice

½ tsp cinnamon

1 whole duck

300g (10½oz) baby carrots, washed and
 larger ones halved

300g (10½oz) baby parsnips, washed and
 larger ones halved or quartered

1 small celeriac (celery root), peeled and
 cut into slim wedges

200g (7oz) kale, tough stalks removed and
 leaves torn

sea salt

FOR THE SPICED ORANGE SAUCE

1 lemon, zest and juice

100g (3½oz/scant ½ cup) granulated sugar

2 tbsp water

300ml (10½fl oz/1¼ cups) orange juice

1 cinnamon stick

1 star anise

2 cloves

50g (1¾oz/3½ tbsp) cold unsalted
 butter, cubed

sea salt

Preheat the oven to 180°C/160°C fan/350°F/gas mark 4. Line a roasting tin with a double layer of foil and place a trivet on top.

Mix the five spice, cinnamon and 1 teaspoon of crushed sea salt together in a little bowl. Rub the mix all over the duck and place it on the trivet. Pop it into the preheated oven for 2½ hours. Turn once halfway through cooking.

After 1½ hours, the duck will have rendered a huge amount of its fat, which will have collected in the foil liner. Spoon 2 tablespoons of that fat into another roasting tin. Put the carrots, parsnips and celeriac into the tin and shake the tray to coat them with the duck fat. Season and pop them in the oven on the shelf below the duck for the last hour of cooking, shaking again after half an hour.

Continued overleaf

SHREDDED DUCK, ROAST ROOT VEG, KALE & SPICED ORANGE

To make the sauce, first peel the lemon zest off in big strips and juice the lemon. Then, put the sugar and water in a saucepan over a medium heat. The sugar will start to dissolve and then melt. Don't be tempted to stir, just swirl every now and again to keep it cooking evenly. Keep going until the sugar goes golden brown – like caramel. At this point (carefully) add the orange and lemon juices – do be careful as it will sizzle and spit. The sugar may harden but it will re-melt as the juices warm up. You can stir gently and encourage it to dissolve. Add the strips of lemon zest, along with the spices and leave to infuse and reduce over a low heat for 30 minutes.

Meanwhile, place the kale leaves into a mixing bowl along with half a teaspoon of crushed sea salt. Massage the salt into the leaves with your hands for a few minutes – you should find that the kale will suddenly go much softer. Leave to one side until you're ready to serve.

When the duck is cooked, remove it from the oven and leave to rest for 10 minutes. Check the root veg are done and remove them as well.

Take the sauce off the heat once it has reduced by around half its original volume. Remove the zest and spices and discard. Add the cubes of butter one at a time, whisking to incorporate them into the sauce as you go. It should be smooth and glossy and beautifully perfumed. Taste and add a pinch of salt to help balance the sweetness.

Lay the kale leaves on the base of a serving platter and top with the roasted root veg. Shred the duck with two forks and pile all over the veg. Drizzle over some of the sauce and serve the rest on the side.

This is joyous.

ROAST CHICKPEAS & PEPPERS WITH WARM CHILLI TAHINI (VG)

This is a delightful one-tray salad, which goes from oven to table, so it is super-simple to make – and wash up! As it's a warm salad with hearty flavours and a little heat I think this makes it perfect, veggie-packed comfort food.

1 red (bell) pepper, deseeded and chopped into chunks

1 orange (bell) pepper, deseeded and chopped into chunks

1 yellow (bell) pepper, deseeded and chopped into chunks

2 red onions, peeled, chopped into chunks

700g (1lb 9oz) jar of chickpeas (garbanzo beans), drained and rinsed (about 540g/1lb 3oz total drained weight)

1 garlic bulb, broken into cloves, peeled and lightly bashed

3 tbsp olive oil

1 tbsp sweet smoked paprika

1 tbsp dried oregano

1 tsp chilli flakes (crushed chilli)

100g (3½oz) baby leaf spinach

40g (1½oz) rocket (arugula)

sea salt and freshly ground black pepper

FOR THE CHILLI AND TAHINI DRESSING

2 tbsp tahini

4 tbsp sweet chilli sauce

3 tbsp water

1 tbsp light olive oil

TO SERVE

handful of flat-leaf parsley leaves

handful of dill leaves

chilli flakes (crushed chilli)

Preheat the oven to 190°C/170°C fan/375°F/gas mark 5. Put the peppers, onions, chickpeas and garlic in a roasting dish that you can take straight to the table. Add the olive oil, paprika, oregano and chilli and some seasoning. Toss everything together.

Roast in the preheated oven for 20 minutes, then remove, turn everything over and return to the oven for another 20 minutes.

Meanwhile, make the dressing. Place all the ingredients into a saucepan over a low heat. Whisk to bring it together while it gently heats through. I like my dressing relatively thick so 3 tablespoons of water is usually enough for me, but if you like it thinner, add more, another teaspoon at a time.

When the veg is all deliciously squashy with some crispy edges, remove from the oven. Allow to cool for a few minutes and then stir in the spinach and rocket leaves. Drizzle over some of the dressing and serve the rest on the side. Garnish with some fresh herbs and an extra sprinkle of chilli flakes.

THINGS TO KNOW

To make sure you get the very best results from your Big Salads when you make them, here are just a few little tips and tricks to help you with some of the elements.

For example, I love to use nuts and seeds to finish a salad – not only do they add some crunch and texture but they can add another level of flavour. Toasting them can make those flavours even more dynamic. I like to do them in the oven as I think it makes for a more even way of cooking and you don't run the risk of charring bits, as you do in a dry frying pan. By toasting big batches of nuts and storing them in airtight containers you'll always have them to hand when you need them – plus they make for healthy snacks or a topping on your breakfast – so that's a win win!

TOASTING NUTS

Preheat the oven to 190°C/170°C fan/375°F/gas mark 5. Place the nuts in a single layer over the base of a large-lipped baking sheet or roasting tin. Pop them into the oven for 8 minutes. Remove from the oven and shake them around, moving the outer ones in as they tend to toast more quickly around the edges. By this point, they should be starting to turn golden brown. Return to the oven for another 6–10 minutes to fully toast them. Blanched hazelnuts, almonds, flaked almonds and pine nuts tend to take the least time, while larger nuts like pecans and walnuts etc can handle a little more time in the oven.

TOASTING SEEDS

Follow the nut method above (same oven temperature and single layer on a baking sheet) but increase the cooking time to 10 minutes before you give them their first shake. Then return to the oven for another 10–12 minutes. If you're toasting sunflower seeds, the outer skin will start to pop open; sunflower seeds will become slightly golden.

KITCHEN KIT

You don't need to have lots of fancy kit to make the recipes in *Big Salads*. A normal home cook should have enough pots and pans and baking sheets to create all these recipes at home. However, if I could recommend just two pieces of equipment that would save you time, they would be an adjustable mandolin and a mini-chopper.

Mandolins make slicing things like fennel, beetroot (beets), shallots, radishes, cabbages (and so much more) a great deal faster – plus they keep everything lovely and even, without relying on your knife skills, which helps your finished dish to look amazing. Having an adjustable mandolin means you can vary how thinly you can slice, so you get the fruit or veg just how you like it.

A mini-chopper is great for making some of the dressings or pestos, for roughly chopping nuts, making pastes etc. I couldn't live without mine – after all, the quicker I am in the kitchen, the more fun I get to have with my guests.

I mention using cast-iron frying pans (skillets) and griddles, too, and while these can add to the effect of a dish, if you don't have one a normal frying pan will be just fine. Don't be deterred – where there is a will, there is always a way!

INGREDIENTS AND SOURCING

The majority of the ingredients used in these recipes should be readily available, no matter where you live, from your local supermarket, corner shop, fishmonger, butcher or greengrocer. However, there may be a few things like Korean glass noodles, fresh anchovies or octopus that might be slightly harder to find. As a food writer, I don't ever want people not to be able to make my food (otherwise, what's the point?), so I'm hoping these websites may help you source a few of the ingredients that aren't always in every supermarket.

souschef.co.uk
frozenfishdirect.co.uk
kingcrab.co.uk
ocado.co.uk
freshdirect.com
instacart.com
wholefoodsmarket.com
amazon.com

I always use Maldon sea salt flakes, so if you use a different kind of salt please adjust the amount accordingly. You'll need far less of a fine salt. Seasoning a finished dish is also a very personal thing, so always season to taste – just remember you can always add more but you can't take it away.

I always use free range eggs from high-welfare, happy chickens. They just taste better.

I try to buy the best-quality produce that I can afford and use it lovingly. Try finding a local butcher and fishmonger for good-quality meat and fish. Many of the recipes are plant-based so when adding meat and fish, try and make it count if you can.

STORAGE
Most dressings and sauces will keep for at least a few days if stored in a clean, airtight container in the fridge. Herb-based dressings may become a little less vibrant but no less tasty, just shake well before using them again to make sure everything gets re-mixed.

LEFTOVERS
Love them.

ACKNOWLEDGEMENTS

The first of my thanks must go to the wonderful team at Quadrille, headed up by the mighty Sarah Lavelle, for giving me this incredible opportunity. I've worked on countless books and magazines and within publishing for many years, so to have my own cookbook is a dream come true. From the bottom of my heart, I thank you. I hope I have done *Big Salads* justice and brought the dream to life.

To Catherine Frawley, a photographer extraordinaire, and someone who I am so pleased to now call a friend. You've left me speechless many times (and this never usually happens) with your beautiful photos and light touch. I am so lucky and grateful to have had you and Michael help make this book something we can all be very proud of. Thank you for letting us take over your home.

Maeve Bargman is the wonderful designer who has brought together the book you hold in your hands, and I hope you agree it's truly a thing of beauty. Thank you for pushing the idea of what a cookbook should look like and for raiding the all-you-can-eat buffet with such enthusiasm at the end of every shoot day – the fact that the size of container increased almost daily made this feeder very happy indeed.

Rachel Vere who took my love of strong graphic patterns and ran with it. You have a fabulous eye for props and my food has never looked so at home in the staggering array of dishes and whopping platters you managed to find! *Big Salads* needed big plates and what beauties you found.

Helen Gatherer – there are no words. I'm struggling to know how to thank you for everything you did for me on this shoot. You are a brilliant, kind and fun person to be around. You kept me going; sang and danced with me as we prepped and cooked, and then cooked some more. And you did it all out of the kindness of your heart. How lucky am I to have met you? Very. Thank you.

Thanks also to Sarah Chatwin for asking all the right questions so nothing was missed or left unexplained and Harriet Webster for coordinating and making sure everything was just where it needed to be!

Thank you to the wonderful St. Ewe Free Range Eggs, who so kindly supplied the incredibly delicious eggs for the making of this book. They are scrumptious, my favourites and look amazing. Thank you all so much!

And I know it's a bit cheesy and I don't want these acknowledgements to be like a bad Oscar speech that runs on and on but I must thank my mum, after all I wouldn't be here without her. I get all my best bits from you – well, perhaps not the love of cooking or broccoli – but certainly the drive, determination and wanting to make everything perfect. You've always told me I could do anything if I worked hard enough and you've always loved, encouraged, listened or just made it possible, whatever the path. I hope I make you proud. I love you.

Thanks to all my family (particularly Matt, Sanida and Oliver) and friends – especially Liz, Emma and Holly who I've known forever – for all the ridiculous laughs and unwavering support. And to everyone else that's part of the ride, I love you all dearly. Now please go and buy lots of copies and spread the love of *Big Salads*.

To my incredible husband, Spencer. I couldn't have done any of this without you. I'm a better person for knowing you. You make me laugh so much. You always have my back (and usually a cold beer) when I need one. You give me the love and confidence to keep pushing on and you are my motivation – you're also a wonderful distraction! Extra-special thanks for being first in line for tasting when I write recipes – I must say you've really taken on that job with gusto! Love you forever. Now, if I can just get you to eat cheese…

And lastly, to all of YOU who have bought the book, who embrace the idea that is *Big Salads* (and are already putting in post-its of the recipes you want to try) … That's what it's all about. THANK YOU.

INDEX

ENJOY!

@KATINTHEKITCHEN